Before/After

Erik Keevan

NEWMAN SPRINGS PUBLISHING
320 Broad Street
Red Bank, NJ 07701

First originally published by Newman Springs Publishing 2021

Before/After Cover design
by Crysta Anne Marie

ISBN 978-1-63692-393-2 (Paperback)
ISBN 978-1-63692-394-9 (Digital)

Printed in the United States of America

This book is dedicated to those that stood by me while I was lost and helped me find my way again. Thank you.

And to those that I hurt when I was broken, I am sorry. I will never be that person again.

Contents

Preface

The original name of this book was "Don't Worry, You're Going to Die." I say original... It was the name that I decided my second book would be after I published *Obituaries for Terrible People*. It fit my dark sense of humor, but with a small touch of hope in it. Like, sad hope, but still hope.

But after my suicide attempt on July 13, 2019, I realized that wasn't me anymore. It was masking the way that I actually felt with this dark humor. Do I still have a dark sense of humor? Sure. But I realized I wasn't being fair to myself by hiding that pain that I felt. I realized that I deserve to be honest with myself about everything that I'm feeling and that my friends and family that had to watch me almost leave their lives deserved to see that honesty as well. And so, I changed my approach.

Before/After is a personal book to me. It's a book about the growth I've gone through since that July day over a year ago. It's a book about reflections and new beginnings. It's about learning from your past and building a better future from it. I've included poetry and stories written before my suicide attempt, and then stories and poetry from after the attempt to juxtapose the mental shift that I've gone through. Friends have told me that my work has become more hopeful. I'll let you decide that for yourself.

I also included personal essays about my change—including steps I've taken in case you're looking for new ideas. Or if you're wondering what it's like in the mind of a loved one who is struggling, or has lost the struggle, with their mental health.

Suicide is something that touches all of our lives. About eight hundred thousand people die of suicide every year. If you're lucky enough to not have known anyone who has committed suicide, you probably at least know someone who is struggling with it. Even if you don't know. And yet, it's still so taboo, still so looked down upon in our society that most people don't feel comfortable talking about it or reaching out when they're struggling. They feel too ashamed, too hurt, too broken to try and talk to others. And even when they do talk about it, people don't know how to listen to the issue and just make things worse.

So that's what this book is. A start to the discussion. I hope that it brings you some clarity, some hope, some comfort in having complicated discussions about mental health. Maybe it will help. Maybe it won't. At the very least, I hope that it will help people realize that they're not alone in feeling like life will never get better. But it does get better. And you can make it better.

And if you can't? At least we can try.

Before

And Thus, I Am a Priest

And thus, I am a priest
wading into the den of sin that is my mind,
armed with nothing more than shots of holy water and a crucifix
in the form of whiskey and a pen.

I Can't Quite See Your Face

I can't quite see your face.
It is smudged,
ink touched before allowed to set.
Your brown eyes shifted to shadow,
and your chin smeared into your neck,
and your hair a cluttered mess of blond and black,
and I can't see you.
I can't see your smile
or your earrings
or your nose,
only the idea that they should be there,
where they once were.
I used to know it so well,
but now I can't quite see your face.

Harvest

I fell in love
under the sunken jaw of the harvest moon,
in front of a million staring eyes.
I lost my mind in the great abyss
and slowly stole my lover's kiss
as she pulled me beneath a flowing skirt
to break a few seconds with her silence.
The festival showered us with
ashen stars;
light danced upon her forehead and down her arms
as I subtly slipped a hand around her waist.
We danced through the night;
sweat dove down my chin
and dripped softly upon her breast
as it heaved heavy with her breath,
as well as her laughter.
The night was torn by our flowing form,
and the hearts of many beat as one,
and slowly, slowly we built together,
fevered and sick and lost our lungs
laughing into the cool night air,
as the moon passed down
a silver crown for my Harvest Queen.

Irish Prozac

I don't need Prozac;
I have whiskey.
It's kind of the same thing,
only it makes me hate myself more,
so I have to be better.
I have to be better now,
because I know if I'm not,
the bad about me will outweigh the good,
and I've been there before.
I nearly died there before.
And so I know I can't go back there.
Not now.
Not tomorrow.
So I'll be my best now, and I'll hate myself later,
and hope I can convince myself
that I'm worth saving.

Me Vs. the Butcher

I am nothing more than the flesh on my bones,
and I mean nothing more than the cow,
fighting uselessly as he is pressed onto the slaughter floor.
One day, the hammer will fall on the base of my skull,
and my life will collapse into
a body again,
and I will finally have purpose as food for the meal worms in my eyes,
and the flies that flit upon my blood-covered arms.

But for now, I am less than a body,
and purposelessly, I will fight as best I can against the
coming of the hammer.
One day I will lose,
but that doesn't mean I'm going to make it easy
on the butcher.

I'm Sorry, Charlie, but There's a War On

"**D**rink this," the man set a small glass of what looked like whiskey but smelled like gasoline, in front of me.

My whole body was sluggish, my head ten feet removed from my body, or so it felt. I could hardly squeeze out the single sentence "Where am I?"

"It'll come to you. Drink."

I did as I was told. My fingers were hardly able to close around the glass, felt bruised, but I was able to bring the glass to my mouth. The cheap whiskey burned the back of my throat. At least I knew I was alive. I put the glass back on the table with a clunk.

I tried balling my hand into a fist, but my fingers would hardly move. Swollen, puffy, and sore, my fingers just sat uselessly extended.

I looked around for the first time and found that I was sitting in a wooden chair, pulled up to a small bar table. The air was musty and clung to my skin; cigarette smoke settled over everything. There was only one light, hanging harshly above my head, making my eyes sting. If there was anyone in the room besides myself and my bartender, I couldn't tell. Three empty glasses sat on the table in front of me.

The man drew a chair to the far side of the table and sat down. As he sat down, he flashed a forced smile at me.

"Now, Charlie, what do you remember?"

The numbness of my body was finally receding, illuminating the pain radiating through my body. A dull ache in the base of my skull spider cracked its way through my body. My joints were stiff, and my muscles were enflamed. So that was why I couldn't close my fist.

I vomited, hard, over the side of the chair. The man across the table sighed.

"Charlie. Charlie! Pull yourself together. Think. Think, what did you see?"

My head pounding, I tried to remember a few moments before. My head swam, and then a memory that wasn't mine floated into my head. No, that wasn't exactly right. Then a memory that hadn't happened yet floated into my head.

It was a newspaper, I could tell that. But the memory was fragmented, like the reminder of your first steps. There was a picture on the front page, large and cluttered. Rubble of buildings, firemen standing in the ruins and dust, pulling bodies from underneath. Not all of them looked alive.

"There's a newspaper. Some...attack."

"We know that, Charlie. We know that. Where? Can you see where?"

I try remembering this future memory. A newspaper being held in front of me.

Hands...the hands holding it in front of me... I'm sitting at the same table that I'm sitting at now. And the man holding it...the same man who is across from me now. Only, he has a bandage on his head, covering his eye. He's shouting at me, but I can't make out what he's trying to say. Just...white noise.

My head drops and almost hits the table as a wave of exhaustion rolls over me. Nausea flashes behind my eyes.

"September 11, 2001." I remember the date from the upper right-hand corner of the paper.

"We know the date, Charlie. We need to know who. And where. Focus."

I think. I remember what hasn't happened yet. I see the paper, and the man, and I focus, hard, I try to see...

And then I'm pushing through the paper-thin future memory and arrive in an actual memory. I see my wife in a white dress. Our wedding day. And at the same time, superimposed, half-written over that memory, our bodies together. I can taste her skin, she consumes me. I follow her memory into myself.

"My wife," I say, lost in memory.

I remember the men who arrived in suits. Doctors and…other men. This man, before me. I remember his name. Carmichael. Agent Carmichael. I remember them knocking on my door. Telling me… telling me that I have a brain defect. No, not defect. Mutation.

How long ago? Months? Years? It's so hard to remember, to focus. I don't even see the sun…

"How long have you…had me here?" I manage to ask, laboring over each word.

The man in front of me sits back in his chair. It creaks against his weight.

They've had me here, however long, sitting in this room. They show me newspapers each day, ask me to remember. To remember things that have never happened.

"My wife. I want to see my wife."

The man leans toward me, his smile is gone, and I can hear sincerity in his voice.

"I'd like nothing more than to send you home to your wife, Charlie," he begins. "Trust me. But your brain… You're the only one who can do this. The only one. And we need this, we need you. I wish we didn't, but we do."

The man gestures to someone behind me, someone I can't see. I hear footsteps, and I try to turn, but my body is too exhausted. I feel two strong hands on my shoulders.

"I'm sorry, Charlie, but there's a war on," the first man says.

There is a blinding pain as the person behind me stabs something into the base of my skull. The room dissolves around me…

And there I am, once again sitting in the same room, and the man is sitting before me holding up a newspaper, trying to tell me something. Something important. He has bandages on his head, covering his eye, but I know him.

I remember this.

Cuts

The night is cold,
but the blood is warm,
so he cuts,
cuts,
cuts
to keep himself from freezing to death.

The Lifecycle of Fireflies

The fireflies vomited up their light bulbs,
and now all that are left are maggots
squirming in my eyes at night.
They slither and turn and vacate their twisting places
and find themselves alive,
dancing upon the corner of my eyes,
and your eyes,
and the eyes of everyone who ever felt alive.

I collected the light bulbs,
and twisted them into my blistering flesh,
straight into the blood
and sinew that I call my body.
And I burned.
I burned with such vision
that maybe I lit the way for one person,
or two people,
or, if I'm lucky, even three.
I burned my life right down to the fireflies
in the hope that I might one day
turn into maggots
to feast on the eyes
of someone who might see.

Six Feet Three Inches

What is the funeral song for?
Why have I spent so many useless nights
spinning words in my head
for nothing?
I can see now.
Finally I can see,
and I see myself alone
in a sea of endless grief.
But I am not grief.
Is grief what people saw?
No, I am love
and peace
and harmony,
despite what everyone saw in me.
And yet,
as they lower me in six feet down
(well, to be honest, it was six feet and three inches,
but I'm the only one who is counting)
all they remember is the grief.

I'm sorry,
all I was trying to do was save you.

Pies

My grandmother is,
quite frankly,
losing her mind.
They say it's not Alzheimer's,
but still she slips slowly down the slope of senility,
away from the woman I remember from my childhood.

She's far from the only one,
far from the only grandmother to lose the thread of reality.
But, selfishly, I feel...
she's mine.
She's my grandmother.

She hasn't forgotten me.
Yet.
But she just forgot the recipe for my favorite pie.
The pie she would make me every Christmas,
every Thanksgiving,
every Easter.
Sure, other people ate it, too,
my cousins and uncles and aunts...
but she always made it for me.
She taught me,
when I was old enough to learn how to cook for myself,
how to make the pie,
so that every Christmas,
and every Thanksgiving
and every Easter,
I could make it for our family.
But now she's forgotten how to make it.

And so I'll sit here, now,
thousands of miles away from her home,
and my home as a child,
while her mind softly slips away,
and the handwritten notes in her birthday cards slowly
disappear a little more every year
until it is nothing more than a signature.

Well,
at least I still remember how to make the pie.

Places I Never Thought I Knew

I heard a story when I was a child.
I think my mother spoke it to me.
But that is unimportant.
I heard a story, and I found there
living between the words
a life that breathed as true as I.
And I fell in love.
The story swept and folded
and mapped and drew
and dreamt.
Mostly it dreamt.
It was all that I had,
and it is all that I have ever carried with me.
Not the words,
no,
the words are as unimportant as who spoke them.
But the breath the story blew
has carried my mind
to places that I never thought I knew.

My Home and the Sea

I think if I was born a hundred and fifty years ago,
I could have been a sailor,
borne on the sea with salt in my hair
and adventure etched in ink upon my skin.
A map of stars and sea monsters and mermaids
navigating me through the open world,
and beyond.
I could have sailed right over the edge of the world
and down, down, down into the depths of hell
and carried back with me the spirits of my ancestors,
matched each heartbeat to the ebb
of the sea against the wood beneath my feet.
I would be owned by Poseidon and Triton,
and when my mortal form had decayed and rotted,
my soul would be claimed,
and I would live forever,
placed in the very sea foam I call home.

But I was not born a hundred and fifty years ago.
I was born to the age of computers and airplanes,
not of grand adventure and sea ships.
And now the closest that I come to the sea
that floods through my veins,
is lying on my waterbed
and wearing a papier-mâché captain's hat
that I made as a child.

Secondhand Heart

I bought a heart with the last pennies in my pockets.
It wasn't a perfect heart,
it was second hand
and had a patch sewn on the left ventricle,
but it was mine.
Together that heart and I loved,
loved brightly and haphazardly,
imperfectly,
unaware
or uncaring,
of what it might cost.
It walked me through nights,
and kissed me through days,
wrapped me,
until eventually it went away,
and my heart forgot that its purpose was to love.

I sold my heart for the last pennies to my name.
It helped me buy a bottle and a record player.
It isn't a perfect heart,
there is a patch on the left ventricle
and another on the third chamber,
but it isn't mine.
Not anymore.
Maybe another mind can remind it
how to be happy.

Self-Harm—Essay

While I was in the hospital last year, and then discussions with my psychiatrist and therapist afterward, I came to the realization that I didn't only have depression but also had really bad anxiety. Like, really bad. Which was strange to me, since some things didn't seem to bother me too much in the way that anxiety is normally manifested. Like I didn't get test anxiety (though that might have just been me shutting down). In retrospect, I was just manifesting it in different ways, which is why I'm now on an anti-anxiety medication (and why I stopped drinking coffee, and *damn* what a difference that made).

It explained a lot about why I liked drinking. Because a lot of those horrible effects of anxiety, like heart racing, circular thinking, etc., were fixed when I'd drink. It would let me feel normal for a bit (until, on the other side, it got *way* worse). I spent so long talking about how depressed I was that I failed to notice how anxiety was working hand in hand with it. I was trying to balance in the middle but instead kept seesawing from one to the other.

It also explains the worst side effect of my mental health issues that I tried silencing with alcohol (and which was also often made *worse* by alcohol… I was real dumb, what can I say?) This part is kind of graphic, so feel free to skip this paragraph and start again with the next piece. When I would get overwhelmed with depression and anxiety, I would become extremely aware of my veins. They would start to almost burn, and I'd want to literally rip them out. It was overwhelming and extremely hard for me to resist. I'd feel like I'd never let go of that feeling. Like I just wanted to take something and dig them out of my body so that I'd stop feeling it. It was something that had been around for a while but had gotten worse in the last few years due to my descent into alcoholism and shutting myself off more and more from the world. I know everyone is aware of my attempt last summer, but what very few people are aware of is I had two near attempts in the years leading up to that, including the night of my book release party for *Obituaries for Terrible People*... hence why I ended up distancing myself from it and stopped writing for years.

I struggled with self-harm since I was a teenager. Started with me hitting myself and hitting my head against things. Then it grew into razors, knives, etc. I never talked to anyone about that, even my college therapist (yay CAPS) because I was too worried about what that would mean about me. And I actually *had* stopped doing that for a few years before last summer. I had moved past it, and somehow in my mind, I thought that not cutting myself meant that I was getting better. But I was really just shifting it into drinking instead, which was damaging myself in a different way. It was just the next evolution of my self-harm.

The week leading up to my attempt, I relapsed on self-harm. I carry a knife around with me for protection, probably not the best thing for someone with as severe of depression as I had. But I started cutting on my ankles that week (that way it was easy to hide). It was the first time I had done it in about six years. I was hoping that it would be enough to stop my suicidal thoughts, but it wasn't. I had just slid so far down that I was too lost even for that.

I don't say any of this to dwell. My anxiety has been so much better, and I haven't wanted to do anything to my veins. Nowhere near a cutting relapse. My worst days now are, mentally, the same as my best days before (maybe not best best, but like the good days when my mind would still go to a dark place). I spent so long trying to have my partners fix that broken part of me that I never actually did anything to fix it myself. I just sank lower and lower into it. It's a slippery slope that you don't even realize you're on until it's gotten bad, and then you just view anyone who points it out to you as critical of you and that just makes it worse. Someone else can't make you realize your own problems.

If you're in this place now...whether it's drug or alcohol abuse, cutting, hitting, angry outbursts, anxiety that makes your skin crawl...whatever it is...just know you're not alone. There are so many of us out there just trying to find peace, and we grab on to anything to try making the pain go away for just a little while. It's okay to want that. But talk to people around you and find a way to find that peace without the self-destruction. You've survived. That's amazing and takes so much strength. But now that you've survived, let's try getting you to a place where you get to live.

The Beauty in Dreams

I realized the beauty
in the fucked-up dreams
that my mind,
long eaten away by illness,
has.
I saw beasts of splendor,
and horror,
and I fell in love with the very monsters
that hold me down.
I found a princess draped
in red cloth,
not red due to the pigment in the fibers,
but rather
the leaking in my mind.
And I found her laid there,
with such delicacy,
that I thought ill to disturb her rest.

So lay easy,
love,
that you may find the beauty
in whatever fucked-up dreams
may fall on your brow.
And I will collect those dreams,
and I will catalogue them in my mind
so that you need not carry them alone.

The Bird's Freedom

The Bird, a bald eagle, sits
perched upon a tree overlooking the arid land,
and he is free as far as his eyes can see.
But beyond the stretch of his eyes,
an unimaginable distance away,
perhaps, even, in another land,
stands the massive wall of a cage.
And behind him, some many miles,
sits another hulking wall.
And on both sides are others,
silver monoliths made of chain and history
keeping The Bird locked within.
And there is a roof, made of the same material,
so that no matter how high The Bird aims,
he shall forever be locked inside.

Now, he can still fly as fast
and as far as he desires.
If he flew all day today and all day tomorrow,
he would not reach the far side
of the cage.
But if he flew for a third day,
oh, the third day.
But the world is his, he tells himself,
and he tells himself that he is free,
for he IS free to do whatever he wishes
within his cage.
But he is not free to leave.
And on days when the sun shines brightest
The Bird can still see the pattern of the cage
reflected beneath him as a shadow.

One More Drink

Let me drink.
Another drink and I'll be fine.
No, Josh, I'll be fine to get home,
it's okay.
I've done this before.
I haven't had that much,
I swear.
One more drink.
One more drink
and finally, this should all be put to rest.
One drink and then I'll walk home.
No, no,
I'm fine.
I swear.
I just need one more drink.
One more drink to feel fine.

Thanks.

My Social Anxiety and Why I Love to Party

I was too trapped in my own head to go out to parties
or clubs
or anywhere, really,
so I threw my own
to feel more normal.
And they came,
my friends,
one after another
and week after week,
and I didn't feel so alone with all my friends around me,
and they didn't feel alone with all of us around them,
and we laughed,
and we cried,
and we drank,
(God, how we drank when we were young)
and we kept each other alive.

Thank you.

Cross My Heart and Hope

I was a child back then.

Hell, I'm still a child, just at an age where other people do not view it of me. But I have to still be a child. Adults aren't scared of things that happened when they were a child, right? So I must still be one; my body just forgot.

We lived, my mom and dad and I, in a stately white house on the top of a slight green hill. An immense oak sat at the cusp of the hill, right next to the house, and the pavement of our driveway snaked down to the road below. Since we moved, the street has broken down, tattered and faded memory of my childhood, but back then it was fresh painted and bright.

It was late at night when I was ten. I remember my father was out of town for a seminar in Boston, but I don't remember what the seminar was about. It wasn't a detail that my ten-year-old mind decided was important. That left just my mother and I home alone for three days. It was the second. She had put me to bed at my bedtime, which was nine o'clock. She tucked me into bed and set a small travel clock next to the bed, as she always did, because the ticking helped me fall asleep. Tick. Tick. Tick. Tick.

That is the end of the facts from that night.

I woke up, and it was dark. Very dark. I woke up because of the silence. The clock next to my bed had stopped ticking.

Stupid batteries, I thought and pulled myself out of bed. I fumbled in the darkness, searching the walls for the bathroom door, and I blinded myself as I flicked the light on. In the brilliant flashes behind my eyelids, I relieved myself and then returned myself to the dark.

I knew I wouldn't fall back to sleep without my clock, and I knew that the clock wouldn't work without new batteries. But I knew where I could get batteries. So I journeyed down the dark hallway (here there was at least a little streetlight flitting through the second story window) toward my parents' bedroom.

This late, my mother would be asleep. Asleep and I could slip in and reach high, high, high up onto the bureau and pull down the basket of batteries that she kept there. I was always quiet on my feet... She wouldn't even know I was there.

I twisted the doorknob slowly, grimacing at the sound of the pin scraping against the lock. As I pushed the door open, I held my breath so that the door wouldn't creak. And I was in luck, it swung open soundlessly in the dark in front of me.

In my parents' room, there were four windows spaced evenly across the far wall, and light from the streetlamps always flooded in. My mother typically drew heavy black curtains across them to sleep. But when I entered, they were pulled open, and my mother was pacing in front of them. She was also lying on the bed.

I still don't know if it was on purpose. I never will. The doctor said she had had a couple too many sleeping pills, but it was more the reaction with the alcohol than the pills themselves, so she could have just been trying to sleep. I like to think she was just trying to sleep.

Either way, my mother was lying on the bed, holding a closed bottle of sleeping pills in one hand. A half-empty bottle of vodka sat on her nightstand. She was wearing her pink silk night gown, but she was still wearing her white socks. I still see those white socks. Her eyes were staring up at the ceiling looking for some answer, but she never got one. She just kept asking.

My mother in front of the window turned to me and smiled, a smile that didn't curl up to her nose.

"Honey, did I wake you?"

"The clock stopped."

"Oh... I guess the batteries died, too."

"Why are you two?"

"I'm not. Not anymore. That was just my shell... I don't need it anymore."

"But I liked it. It was pretty."

She smiled again; this one went a little higher.

"I liked it too, sweety. And my life with you and your father... I liked that, too. But it's time for me to go back."

"Go back where?"

"Everywhere," she said, vacantly. She looked out the window at the streetlamp. It glowed back at her.

"I still have a little while. Do you want to sit with me?"

I nodded, and she ushered me onto the bed. She moved her body's legs aside to make room, and we reverently sat on the edge of the mattress.

"Mommy, I don't think I understand?" Even at ten, I was too old to call her mommy…but it seemed like the right word for the occasion.

"I don't either. Not really. Not yet. I'm starting to remember a bit. I know that she's coming, and when she does, I will be gone, but still here, and everywhere. I remember that I promised. We all promised. And she promised us in return. She'll be back to fulfill her promise now. I didn't think it would be this soon."

She held me and put her cheek into my hair, crying. I was used to crying to my mom, not the other way around. It was awkward.

"But I want you to stay, Mommy."

"I want to too, honey."

"So why don't you? Tell her to come another night. Or another year, that would be even better."

"It doesn't work like that. I would stay if I could, but I don't have a choice. We don't get to choose. She just comes and then you know. You remember. You'll remember one day. Hopefully not any time soon."

I didn't understand. I still don't understand; I don't know what promise she made. I know I never made any promise. I started to get scared, and my fear turned to anger, and I bit it, and it spilled into my mouth.

"Well, you can't! I won't let you! I need you. I need you now! You need to stay here. Why can't you be a good mother like all of my other friends' moms and stay here. You're a bad mother leaving me! You're a bad mother!"

Her sobs stopped me; my voice caught, a snowflake on my tongue, melting.

She was doubled over on the bed, her arms pulled tight around her head, and she was rocking back and forth slightly with her sobs.

"I'm… I'm sorry, Mommy," I said, as I slid over to her and shakily put my hands on her shoulder, like I had seen my dad do once when she was upset. "You aren't a bad mommy. You're the best mommy. I promise. Cross my heart and hope to die."

"It's okay, Johnnie." She looked up now, and her face was red, and she sucked air through her nose, a thick snotty sound. "I'm not sad because of you. It's just… I wanted more. I wanted to bring you to the park again. I wanted to give you your first car. I wanted… I wanted more. I am a bad mommy. You're right."

"But you're not a bad mommy." I hugged her. She hugged back, tighter than she had ever hugged me before. "Just don't leave."

"I have to, Johnnie. But I'll… I'll still be here. In a way. I'll be everywhere. And I'll be watching, okay. I'll be watching you on your bike and at school and when you get married…" Her voice broke again, and she glanced threateningly at the window.

"And I'll see you again one day, John. I promise. One day, we can be everywhere together, and we can see the world just like I always told you we would. I promise."

The light coming through the window was brighter now, and I could see the corners of her eyes stretching into crows' feet, and her face folded, defeated. She looked older in that moment than I had ever seen her.

"I love you, Mommy."

"I love you, too." And she hugged me, on her knees, holding on to me as an anchor.

"You be good, okay. You be good for Daddy. He's going to need it. You're gonna have to be a strong little boy. And I know you can do it. Because you are a strong little boy. And I am so, so proud of you. Cross my heart."

And the light was brighter and brighter. It was too bright. I wanted someone to turn out the light. It was going to hurt me. I was going to go blind. I hated it. I could feel the light slither into my eyes and my mouth and my ears, and for a moment, light was all I was. And then the weight of my mother's arms was off me, and I was standing alone in the dark, and I couldn't remember why I was there. The remembering would come later, after the funeral.

I stumbled back to my bed, through my parents' room (though, now it was only my father's room, and he wasn't there), down the hallway which got darker and darker with each step, until I collapsed onto my bed with the race car sheets.

I fell asleep almost immediately. But in the few seconds before I drifted off to sleep, I realized my clock was ticking. Tick. Tick. Tick. Ti...

I wake up and it's light out. Late morning light and birds are singing their bird song. I don't remember my dream from the night before. I don't remember anything. All I have is the light and the birds and the...and the clock, ticking next to me.

I get out of bed, but I don't hear my mom downstairs. I don't hear anything. It's silent.

I walk down the hall and push open her door, and there is my mother, same as the night before, lying in the bed with a bottle in her hands, her legs pushed aside to allow someone to sit on the edge. She is still asking the ceiling her questions.

I call my dad on his cell phone (and back then those were new) because I didn't know what else to do. He tells me to go down and make myself a sandwich and that he is coming home early and to wait for Grammy.

A half an hour later, my grandmother's hulking rust-colored Suburban pulled up the driveway. She came in and hugged me and sat me down in front of the television and went upstairs. When she came down, she was crying. She made herself a sandwich and sat in front of the television with me.

Men in white coats came and took my mother away. But I knew it wasn't her. It was just her shell. They brought a large stretcher up the stairs, strapped her body to it, covered her in a sheet, and brought her back down. They had difficulty getting around the sharp bend at the bottom of the stairs. They pushed and lifted for five minutes, and the sheet fell away. That's how I know they had strapped her down. Then they wheeled her out and into a large van.

My dad got home not long after that. He made sure Grammy was okay and then left again. His face was red and puffy.

It was a long day. And everyone seemed to want to talk to me, but nobody did. I don't know if they would have known what to say, anyway.

The funeral was four days later. Everyone was wearing black. I just wanted some color. Even just a splash. My mother would have wanted that. And that day, everyone had something to say to me. But nobody said anything right. It was all "I'm so sorry for your loss" and "She was a good woman." But none of it meant anything. Vacant apologies.

After the service, my little cousin asked if I wanted to play capture the flag. That was the first right thing anyone said to me. We played, running between tomb stones and across the grass. It was prefect. It was normal.

And that was the end. After that, she was put in the ground, and the story of my mother ended. She was dead and covered in dirt. And eventually I remembered. I remembered the dream that I had had that night. Of my mother's goodbye. And I liked it. Because in the dream, she got to actually say goodbye. She didn't just leave. Because from what I remember of my mother, she would never have just left without saying goodbye. So the dream is nice.

It had to be a dream, right? Those feelings of closure only ever happen in stories and dreams. Life is more complicated, and you never get to say goodbye.

But there are nights, when I see the streetlight flowing into my bedroom, that I cross my heart and hope.

Coke Bottle

Slither and slip
the pill into the coke,
got everything you need to feel as good as you could,
just drink it down,
drink it down,
drink it down they said…
I can't seem to swallow now,
all these years later, the thing
they shoved down my throat,
even now that it's gone.
And I don't know why, and I don't know way,
but the coke that I drank seems to have stayed
inside me.

Happiness

I didn't find happiness here.
I didn't find happiness there.
I didn't find happiness anywhere.
I didn't find happiness up.
I didn't find happiness down.
I didn't find happiness anywhere.
And here I am,
a depressed Dr. Seuss,
standing star bellied
at the bottom of an empty glass.

I Can't Think of a Title for this Poem, Due to the Abrasive Nature of Its Contents

If I died tomorrow,
I don't think anyone would be surprised.
Sad, yes,
my depression is not so bad right now to think that no one cares,
but surprised, not so much.
My struggle with my own mind is visible enough that I think
I'm the only person I actually fool when I say,
"I'm fine."
I mean, hey, whatever, I do it for my writing.
For my passion.
For the world.
Whatever excuse I use.
But there are times when I think that it would be lovely
if I could simply let it all go
and live a normal life with a normal mind
and normal happiness.
And I realize that there is nothing that is truly
"normal happiness."
But a man can dream, can't he?
And then I see a friend struggle and fall
and slip into habits that I, too, have,
and I realize that no matter what trauma I put myself through,
the words I might pass to them are worth
the damage they might do to me.

And so tonight, I will drink myself to sleep, again,
alone and scared in a broken world.
But for the waste of my life,

and eventual loss of it,
I know that dozens will still stand because of me.
And that's all I need to know.

I think.

In Her Eyes

The petals sat delicately in her eyes,
wide pride and everything but lies
reflected in the soft creases beneath her smile
and the wide wonder of her mind.
She spoke through lace of
a place of peace
and time
and hope
and she wrapped me in her cold embrace
to leave me destitute and alone
and vomiting in a gutter filled with pebbles.
And each cut into me with each retch,
spinning and vicious and falling
ever falling,
falling to the Fallen and Forgotten.
And there I found love and life,
among the unloved and unloving,
and I found dreams in those who had lost hope
and survived.
And I survived.
I survived.
I survived.
I swear,
I survived.

It Gets Better

The calendar split open, and I am ninety-three.
I surprised myself by still drawing breath,
and with my gut in my teeth,
I followed my own beckoning hand
into my life.
I found pictures of children on the wall
and a smiling woman beside me,
whose face I did not recognize.
And I looked into my own eyes and found love there.
And I took my hands in mine and told myself,
"Life gets better."
But I still can't remember which of me
said it.

My First Legal Drink

How about some whiskey?
How about some friends?
How about some cigarette conversations?
How about some chocolate bars?
I remember the feeling,
I remember it all.
I was trying to forget.
I was trying to forget,
and now I try remembering
what I was trying to forget.

How about another drink?

The Dust and I

I fell in love with the ashes
swirling at my feet,
around broken square rocks
jutting high into the skyline,
through my own bone and rotten
flesh.
I found myself dancing alone,
dancing alone,
dancing alone,
and I fell in love
with the dust that danced there, too.

A Walk through the City

Concrete monoliths hover over head,
silent specters of a lost civilization.
No sounds,
only the sun and the dust.
Large metal beasts lay dormant
against the side of the still asphalt river.
Nothing breathes.
My feet kick up clouds behind me.
If I look back, I see only my footprints in the dust.
If I look forward, I see nothing.
Nothing but what I have already passed.
The days are long and hot and empty.
The nights are frozen and silent and empty.
I walk with no destination.
I walk to walk.
I walk to live.
I walk because this silent jungle has never been my home.
But my home has been gone for a long, long time,
and all that remains is this empty city.

Where Does My Body Begin?

(Poem written for the short film included in the
compilation *Films Confiscated from a French Brothel*)

WORDS

Why this?

Blindly clinging.
Just blindly clinging.
Driftwood.
Nothing but driftwood
set adrift
and congregating on the waves,
collecting into useless pairs,
a useless mass.
I can't see land anymore.
I can't.
I can't.
It's nothing.
Nothing.
Nothing.
Fine.

WORDS

I'm fine.

I just can't see land.
But that's fine.
That's fine.
Driftwood.
Clinging,

useless,
useless,
uselessly clinging.
                    WORDS
                                   What time is it?
When is it?
When is this?
A moment.
Just a moment.
But it's the moments,
the moments,
that turn into seconds,
into deaths,
every second into more deaths,
and I wait.
Why is that?
I wait and she waits,
and she waits and I wait with her,
wait for her to wait,
time eating away at my skin,

WORDS
                              rotting it,
two pieces of rotting meat left out
decomposing until large chunks of flesh
fall from her stomach and my breast
and my thighs and her neck,
melting wax dripping.
I collect at my own feet.
I collect at her feet,
and she melts at mine.
I can see rib cages,
burning white
burning
burning
burning

WORDS
I feel it burning on my wrists

we're just waiting
and melting
my wrists
my wrists are burning.
Why?
Why this?
Why me?
Why her?
My lungs aren't working anymore.
They just burn.
It's okay,
it's okay,
it's okay.
I'm only burning.

Please don't remember me like this.
Please don't remember me burning.
WORDS

Remember that winter?
The long sleeves covered it.
Out of sight,
it didn't exist.
The burning was the only way to tell,
so I was the only one who could tell.
Can you see it?
Is it obvious?
Should it be covered?
Why did I even?
I can't remember.
But I did.
She's going to ask.
They always ask.
When?
When?

WORDS
When?
It's just a matter of time
Tick
Tick
Tick
Tock,
ask again and ask a lot.
It's how it's always done.
Why hasn't she asked yet?
It's so obvious.
How could she miss it?
I don't know.
Maybe this isn't good enough.
She cut off her tongue and put it between her legs,
and we talked.
We talked all night.
But we haven't talked since.
Not really.
Is it because she saw it?
Can you see it?
Can you see it?
Can you?
I'm burning.
It's burning.

WORDS

Please remember me.

Death Poem

I know not when I'll die,
only that I will.
I do not fear it;
I do not run from it.
There is a piece of me that yearns for the peace,
the comfort,
the freedom of death.
But I do not seek death.
Those who seek death,
oft find it too close to their own hearts.
Instead, I dream,
I love,
I laugh,
I taunt death, on the precipice of life.
So that when my friend,
our oldest friend,
slips into my armchair at night,
I will not fear.
I will not run.
I will arrange my best clothes,
and I will walk into the unknown.

Five or Zero

She had to stop the volume at five or zero.
I remember that—
sitting on the collapsing futon
watching useless television
(useless because how could I pay
attention to the screen when I could look at her face?),
and I would stop the volume wherever it sounded best—
seven, three, nine, wherever.
And she would close her eyes
and not open them until I changed it,
to a five or a zero,
whichever was closer.
Her compulsion,
not mine.
I had enough of my own.

We would watch shows vacantly,
I remember that,
her lying her head in my lap,
me lying my head on her chest,
talking,
making out,
fucking.
Whatever we felt at the time—
but always the TV glowing,
volume set at five or zero,
whichever was closer.
I found her there,
her words and her mind and her pictures and
her compulsions.

And I found myself,
too.
My compulsions and my mind.
I remember that.
I really do.
Because I can't forget.

It's been years now,
since I lost her.
I spend a lot of my days with stoned whiskey,
all my compulsions,
and cheap beer,
the TV glowing in front of me,
set to five or zero.
Always five or zero.

Whichever was closer.

Asleep in the Noon Sun

I never had wings,
so I was never really an angel,
but I have been dead,
with my feet buried deeply in the dirt,
and my arms spread wide to cover you
as you lay upon a small cloth sheet,
asleep in the noon sun.

Cacophony in the Trees

Cacophony
Cacophony
Cacophony
She sang to me,
in the smoke-wood forest
she first bared herself to these eyes of mine.
And I found myself
in attraction's law
when the hands in mine turned to paws,
and she paused to wash her sleek coat
in the creek cut between the wood.
In nothing else
she called to me,
and pulled me forward into a kiss,
a kiss
a kind
a sharing of minds
and laid me down atop the stone-covered beach
to show me the clouds—
and the curve of tree,
and the bend of bow
across the stream,
cut through the trees,
and I watched
and they watched
and she danced atop,
and I saw
but for a moment
myself through the eyes of the trees
and the birds
and the clouds

and the sky.
And when it was done,
we stood and walked,
hand in hand,
through the dense copse of ever greens,
hand in hand
and only ourselves,
as I pulled a tiny pebble from the small of my back.

She Makes My Mind Stop

She makes my mind stop.
And while that may sound terrifying to you,
to me it is a faint hope in a fragile mind.
She curls through my brain like her smoke curls out her car window
and tenderly twists my head until I can breathe
and I can dream
and I can sleep again.
A soothing moment in time.
I find her tears wrapped around mine
and drain and drip upon the flowers below
and they grow, they grow, and grow
and carry me high, high into the sky
until my breath freezes in my chest—

and I find myself still upon my bed,
and her lips have slid past mine.
And I am fine.

The Rectangle and the Circle

The Rectangle looked at the Circle
and said "Oh,
how I wish I could see the world from your view."
And the Circle replied to the Rectangle,
"No, you truly do not.
But only if we were Triangles,
then life would be perfect."

Holy Camera

She holds her camera,
a holy symbol
to remind herself that even on the worst days,
things can still be better,
and so she sits and clicks
clicks
clicks
through the pixels
as the world just shifts around her.

My Night with Death

I had a pint, and he drank a fine red wine.
It was surprisingly civil,
as it turns out.
We sat and talked.
He explained why I couldn't stay.
I agreed.
It was, in the end, my decision.
We played darts,
and I won.
But I think he let me win.
I think he lets everyone win,
in the end.
I think he might be the only person who ever really loses.
I think it's his one last lonely gift
to the only company he ever has.
I think I'd like to see him again, if I could.

But I can't.

Noose Cutters

A *bachelor's apartment. Living room. The room is so clean that it is sterile. A body hangs from a noose in the center of the room. Quiet. Keys jingle and an off-stage door is opened. Two men enter. They are dressed as blue-collar workers—uniforms and such. One of them carries a toolbox. The other carries a large, plastic body bag.*

                          COLIN

Jesus.

                          RAMIEL

What, you got a problem with dead bodies, newbie? You're in the wrong line of work if you do.

                          COLIN

No, I just didn't expect…that. He's just hanging there.

                          RAMIEL

That's why we're here.

                          COLIN

Who found him?

                          RAMIEL

How the fuck should I know?

          RAMIEL pulls out a pack of cigarettes.

Smoke?

COLIN

Can we smoke in here?

RAMIEL

Putting a cigarette in his mouth and gesturing to the body.

Who's gonna stop us? Him?

Sees COLIN's face and puts the cigarette back in the box.

Fine, I won't smoke. All right, kid...

COLIN

Colin.

RAMIEL

Kid, Colin, whatever. I'm not talking to this stiff, so clearly, I'm talking to you. All right Colin, I'm going to get up there and cut him down. You're going to catch him, okay?

COLIN

Yeah. I can do that.

RAMIEL

They're heavier than you think.

RAMIEL opens the toolbox and pulls out a pair of rope cutters. He flips the stool on which the deceased killed himself up and stands on it. COLIN positions himself next to the body.

RAMIEL

Ready?

> COLIN nods. RAMIEL starts using the cutters on
> the rope. After a few hacks, the rope snaps and the
> body falls. COLIN grabs the body but is caught off-
> guard. He wobbles backward and trips. The body
> falls onto a coffee table and smashes it.

RAMIEL

Jesus!

> RAMIEL jumps down. COLIN jumps off the
> ground and runs over to the table.

COLIN

Fuck. I just scratched his face.

RAMIEL

Don't worry about it. Betty can fix it with a bit of makeup when we get back. That's her job.

> COLIN is shaken.

Oh, come on kid. We've all dropped a body at some point or another. They're dead. They can't feel anything. See?

> RAMIEL taps the body with his foot.

Here, sit down.

> RAMIEL sits COLIN down on the couch. He sees
> a minibar and walks over, pours a glass of scotch.

Drink this.

COLIN

I don't feel right drinking a dead man's scotch.

RAMIEL

He doesn't need it anymore. Drink it. It'll help.

> COLIN *takes the drink and sips it, staring at the
> body.*

COLIN

How can you do something like that?

RAMIEL

> *RAMIEL is removing the rope from the ceiling.*

Everyone drops a body every now and then… Nooses are tough.

COLIN

No. I mean suicide. He has to have some family or something.
Friends. What about them? Or the person who found him? They
had to have cared about him…didn't he think of them? How could
he leave them like that?

RAMIEL

He probably cared too much. That's what happens with these people.
But you can't think about all that. It'll drive you crazy. Life is hard on
everyone, Colin. The dead shouldn't be pitied. They aren't victims.
We're just survivors.

COLIN

But they're just…gone.

RAMIEL

That's typically what dying means, yeah. Here, put the rope in the bag.

COLIN

How can this just not phase you?

RAMIEL

Why should it? I've seen dozens of these neck-burners. I've seen gun-
shots, brains just…blam. Hell, one guy basically pulled his veins out
in the bathtub. We all have it in us. We're just the ones who get left
with survivor guilt. That's all your feeling.

COLIN

At least they're somewhere better now.

RAMIEL

Heh. You think? There's nothing out there. This is it. Thankfully.
Only one life to fuck up. Then you're done. Free. Put those cutters
away.

COLIN

How many more of these are we going to get?

RAMIEL

We end up picking up a body every other day or so. People are always
dying, and in a city, well…there are a lot of people. Most of them
are easy—just pick 'em up at the hospital. Some aren't. We get about
a dozen suicides like this a year. Normally overdoses. This one isn't
even that bad. You'll get used to it.

COLIN

I'll never get used to this.

RAMIEL

I said the same thing. You'll be okay. Everyone always remembers
their first.

COLIN

What was yours?

69

RAMIEL

Pours himself a drink. Downs it.

Suicide. Slit wrists.

Beat.

It was my dad.

COLIN
Oh, I'm… I'm sorry… I didn't know…

RAMIEL
Not your fault. Like you said, someone always gets left behind, right?
Now, here…help me get him in the bag.

*COLIN puts his glass down. RAMIEL and COLIN
work together to stuff the body into the body bag.*

RAMIEL
All right, let's get him out to the van. Grab his head.

*The two grab the body bag and start walking it out.
COLIN almost accidentally rams the head into the
couch.*

RAMIEL
Watch it!

The two carry the body offstage.

Beat.

*RAMIEL comes back in. He stares at the empty
apartment. He takes the glasses and moves them to*

the sink. He walks over to where the body was hanging. He stands beneath it for a moment.

He reaches into his pocket and pulls out a crucifix. He lays in gently below where the body was hanging. He crosses himself and lowers his head. Then he exits.

Three Dead Men upon the Tree

There are three dead men,
missing their eyes,
hanging from a tree.
The owl sits there at night,
all seeing from its perch above
the three blind dead men,
and the crows circle high overhead
but never land.
They leave those poor souls alone.

And here is where I find my words,
here beneath an apple tree.
And on that tree rest three dead men
without any eyes.

Perhaps

Perhaps the war is over.
Perhaps the soldiers are all dead.
Perhaps the bodies are buried in one large communal grave,
marked with a white cross and a plaque that says,
"Here I lay my gun, here I lay my head,
and here I lay in silent wake of the living."
Perhaps there is a mass funeral for all sides.
Perhaps I attend.
Perhaps an orator reminds us all that we are nothing but meat,
with beating heart and beating mind
crying against the echoing darkness.
Perhaps we even listen.
Perhaps we remember, and
perhaps we learn.

And perhaps no gun is ever fired again in anger.
Perhaps we live in peace.
Perhaps we live forever.

Perhaps we do.
Perhaps we would.
But we don't.
So pound that bullet into the chamber,
son,
because we need enough soldiers
to fill another communal grave.

After the Dark Comes Up

On the summer eves,
after the dark comes up,
you can find my soul in the clearing of the deepest wood,
dancing with the faerie folk,
exuberant and alive and naked,
among the torch lit tables and the golden platters,
piled high and smelling of sweet meats
and a plethora of spices.

As the crickets draw bows upon their legs
and the fireflies light the floor,
the waltz begins,
and the wraith of my fingers
slip mutely into the delicate hand
of a fair lass,
her amber hair stained black in the flickering shadow
(are her features shifting, or is it just a trick of the light?)
And as we swing through the night
the cascade of music guides our feet,
and our hands,
and our mouths.
We grow close,
but not too close,
our bodies pressed tight but our minds barely scraping.
Her hand is exchanged for another on the floor,
her black hair bleached by sun in the front,
and spinning now,
the lights a blur behind my eyelids,
a sick drunk sound,
and a new pair of hands clasp me firmly, but I spin away,
my feet carrying on ahead of my mind,

and another mouth upon mine,
a fractured senseless mind.
And the fireflies are suns
glowing too hot,
(God, will someone turn the heat down?)
The leprechaun and centaur folk kick and warn,
but the unicorn in his drunk fit
knocks the fireflies from the sky
and they crash among the wood
and the tree faeries flee
as all is consumed by light,
leaving nothing but coals, glowing dull red.

And here is where you can find me,
every night in the summer,
after the dark comes up.

Flowers and Flames

I burned fields of flowers in effigy
of your memory,
cindered petals floated softly on the warm air
as leaves fall in the autumn sun,
and they became your eyes.
Stalks, tarnished black as steel,
grew long, long, long, and
smooth as your legs once were,
and the searing touch of the burning ash
on my bare arm
reminded my skin of your gentle touch,
and I saw you smiling back at me
as the flowers turned into just another field.

I burned fields of flowers in your memory,
and I fell in love with the flames.

The Dead Men Fight

The dead men fight,
bone to bone,
not knowing that they ceased to live
the moment they picked up steel and stone.
And together,
and apart,
they drew their last breaths
through a shaky broken start—
and away they rode,
but stuck at the hip,
bone setting false
and settling through shit
and smoke and dirt and blood
all becoming one upon the sea.
And many dead men gathered on that field
just so that they may see
through judging blind eyes
as they all rush in with a sigh
all bones and all hands and all lives
collect meaninglessly in the dirt as they all die.

Certainty

When I was a kid
I was so certain.
So fucking certain.
Everything I believed was right,
100 percent right.
I knew how to save America,
and myself,
and the lives of those people I loved.
I knew what love was,
and I knew whom I loved.
My mind was so clear,
and my knowledge so vast
that I could do no wrong.

Now...
Now, I honestly don't know.

A Riddle

A neurotic
spread of synapses,
lack of sleep,
forgotten hands,
missing eyes,
cut,
cut again,
dying
but never truly alive.

What am I?

Algae

She was covered in algae
when they found her.
From the sea floor they dragged
her from,
face first and naked
except a thin tin cross necklace
around her neck.
Her eyes were open and clear,
the water faded the blue from her eyes,
a blue that struck everyone
when they saw pictures of her.
Pictures from before,
when she was alive,
anyway.
She's been dead for a long time now.
No one knows why.
No one knows when.
They only know that now she is dead.

And I think I love her.

Happy Ending

I want to give this a happy ending.
But I can't,
because there's not one.

After

One Week Out—Essay

Hi, everyone,

It's been a very long, very odd week for me, and I wanted to kind of debrief everything, for myself as well as for the people in my life.

I'm not sure how apparent it was to everyone. I know Facebook took down the original post, but last Saturday, I became overwhelmed with my depression and all the dark thoughts and attempted to end them in a permanent fashion. Without going into very traumatic details, I'll leave it by saying that what happened was classified a suicide attempt.

When I made the decision to end my life, I was feeling alone, broken, unfixable. I knew there were people who loved me, and there were people that I loved in the world. I knew that there were still good things in the world, things that would make me happy. But that didn't matter to me. All that mattered to me was the pain that I was in and had been in for a very, very long time. My depression had always been a huge part of my life, and for at least the last decade, I haven't been taking the steps I needed to really fix the issues. I just kept putting new half-broken emotions and thoughts on top of each other, pretending that I had done the work required to fix them. Let's just say that doesn't build a good base for anyone's emotional and mental state.

In that moment, I felt everything. I felt all my thoughts, swirling around with the problems in the world right now. Everything just felt so heavy. Heavy enough that some future happiness couldn't be worth dealing with it. I couldn't see an end to that feeling, that super heavy darkness. And all I wanted to do was make it stop. And so I did the one thing I knew would stop it.

I'm lucky that I have so many amazing people in my life, kind people, who reached out. Even though I didn't respond to texts or answer the calls, they gave me back just enough hope to reach out and get in contact with someone who was able to talk me down and to go back home and get the police and medical professionals to me. I'm lucky that I had friends who were willing to come out to try and find me and, once they did, to sit with me to make sure that I was safe.

Looking back, I'm glad that I was admitted to the hospital, even though at the time I really didn't want to be there. It allowed me to have a safe space to process some of the things that I was feeling. There were people there who would just listen and give some ideas for healthy coping mechanisms for how to deal with those thoughts when the world seems like its crashing around you. While I wouldn't recommend it, per se, it wasn't a bad place to be. Everyone was super nice and really wanted to help.

Every day since Saturday has gotten better. By the time I left the hospital, I was in a better place and was enjoying participating in the group sessions. The nurses even said that they were happy I was there because I brought a good energy to the other patients and was able to get people talking about common experiences. I hope that all the other patients that were there with me are able to find the peace they need.

I'm not going to lie, there are still times that I think maybe I should have just gone through with it, that I wouldn't hurt any more if I had. Not that I want to do it at this point, but just the burning question on if it would have been better if I just had. Logically I know it's better now, but there are still moments. Luckily, those moments are getting fewer and further between, especially with the help of all my loved ones that have been helping me.

I've never been good at reaching out. That's half of why last Saturday happened the way it did. If I was better about talking about my emotions, my experiences, and my pain, then I would have been able to make these changes a long time ago. But I'm trying to be better about it. I think that's why I've been so open about everything this week. It's a way to reach out and talk to all of you without reaching out on a personal level, like a halfway point so I don't feel like.

I'm being a burden on anyone. And it's helping me get it out, so that it doesn't just fester under my skin, and I don't end up in the same place I was last weekend. I'm going to start being a much more open and expressive Erik from now on.

It's so odd. Just one week ago, I had been planning on not having a tomorrow. And now that I've gone through that tomorrow, and another, and another I don't fully know where that puts me. It's a weird experience to plan to not be alive and then to find yourself living. But I'm taking every day one at a time and working hard to ground myself in the present through meditation, friends, and lots and lots of music (I've weirdly been in a huge Fall Out Boy phase. Nothing against them, just not the music I expected to be my soundtrack of recovery).

To close, I just want to thank everyone, truly, deeply from the bottom of my heart. If it wasn't for the outpouring of love when I was in my bad mental state or the support I've felt while in recovery, I wouldn't have been able to make it through. So thank you, everyone. Thank you for caring about me, and thank you for giving me a reason to want to keep fighting through all of this.

One Month Out—Essay

Well, it has now been four weeks since I made the decision to end my life. I have spent a lot of time with myself—focusing on me, my well-being, and my mind. I think it's clear that a mind that would come to the conclusion of ending their own life, regardless of their reasoning, is not *well*. But with the work that I've done, with the work that I continue to do, I have grown more than I ever thought possible. Honestly, despite the fact that life hasn't gotten any better, my mind is more at peace than it has been in, well, pretty much my entire life. I've stopped suppressing my emotions, where they then just bubble over as I pretend they don't exist until eventually I explode or breakdown. I've begun allowing myself to experience them. To feel them. To process them in a healthy way and to learn and grow from them.

I'm still not at 100 percent, and I know I still have a lot of work to do to get there. I know it won't be easy work, but I have such a desire to grow and work in a way that I never have before, and I know I will continue to be proactive and help myself be the best person that I can. Not just for myself, but for my friends, my family, for all the people that I love. It's the only way forward: to acknowledge what I've done, the person that I've been, and be a better person than I was. I can't change the past, but I can change my future.

Some of the major changes that I've made in the last month that have gotten me this far:

1) Relying more heavily on talking to my friends about what I'm going through.
2) Allowing myself to acknowledge what I'm going through, what I've been through, and my own responsibility in the things that impact my life.
3) Stopped drinking (though, to be fair, I had done that several months ago).

4) Allowed myself to stop. I always kept myself distracted so that I couldn't dwell or let my mind just be. I always wanted to keep going and do something, needed to do something. But I've started learning to enjoy the silence and quiet times.

5) I've been writing consistently, even if it's not a project. Just getting myself used to getting the thoughts out of my head.

6) Added medication to my preexisting medication. It's all well and good to be doing things to be proactive, but when times are extremely hard, medication will help create a more solid base and allow you the space you need to allow your processes to help.

7) Meditation twice a day, about a half hour a day. I start my day with a ten-minute meditation and end it with a twenty-minute meditation. I use shorter meditations throughout the day if I find my mind is especially turbulent.

8) Being kind to my body. I go to the gym almost every day, eat healthier/protein-filled food. I start the morning with a protein shake with breakfast. Not only has this helped my mind with being grounded, but the physical changes in my body have also helped me feel better about myself. Also has helped my poor tum-tum from feeling awful.

9) I keep myself grounded in the present. I use meditation for this but also have a small medallion I keep in my pocket as a grounding tool. In the worst times, I use the counting grounding mechanism.

10) I've been reading more often, not just absent-mindedly watching TV or playing games. In fact, I've been consuming media more purposefully in general, playing specific games, or watching specific TV shows.

11) I've tried focusing on the good things in my life. It's always been a hard thing for me to do, but I'm being more proactive about appreciating what I have and not dwelling as much on what I don't.

I know that it's not enough to say "I'm better" after doing this stuff for only a month. I'm focusing hard on all this as I move forward, and as time goes on, it'll become more routine, and my mind will reflect that. Like I said, I know I have further to go. But it feels good to be doing things for myself and growing in ways that I never thought I could. I wish I had taken these steps years ago, but I can't change the past. All I can do is take it one day at a time and move forward.

Three Days in a Psych Ward

I never expected to be here,
honestly.
Three days separated from the world
in a sterile cave of
white walls and
an electronically locked door
blocking my exit.
Not that I didn't think I'd need it,
but that I never thought I'd
live long enough
to be here.

I wonder if this is how Jesus felt.

They took my belt,
when I came in,
but not my shoelaces.
They let me keep those.
I still don't know why they
took my belt,
I pointed out to them that
if I still wanted to kill myself,
it would be easy enough to do
with the mirror,
bed sheets,
curtain strings,
sink,
tiles,
plastic knives,
refrigerator,
and so many other items.

If you ever want to piss off a psychiatric nurse,
that's how.

They also took my phone charger.

The walls are white,
like I imagined they would be,
but they're not padded.
The room feels more like a hotel
than a hospital,
except that instead of room service,
I have a nurse who pops her head in the room
every half hour to make sure I'm still alive,
and also I'm not allowed to jack off.
I mean, technically they said no sex,
but I'm assuming the spirit of it covers
self sex as well.

Anyway,
my serotonin is still super fucked
so I probably wouldn't be able to get it up.

Surprisingly,
it's super depressing here.
And quiet.
It feels more like a funeral home
than the usual hustle and bustle
of a hospital.
I met some cool people,
people that seem far more unbalanced than I,
but maybe that's how other people view me as well,
so I don't judge.
They're cool,
but most cool people are at least
slightly unbalanced.

They bring me medicine twice a day,
but I forgot the dosage I take
because my brain was so fogged over,
so they give me twice the usual dose, and it
gives me a headache.

So it goes.

Meals come three times a day.
You get to choose
what you want every night before bed.
And you have to go to
meetings like
four times a day or something.
But at least one of them,
teaches me about meditation,
so it kind of works out.
What would I be doing if I were home,
anyway?
Crying?
I can do that here,
too.

But at least at home, I'd have my cat with me.

My friends come to visit me
the first full day.
We make fun of me trying
to kill myself,
because,
well,
it was SO me.
I wonder if the psych ward
is used to boisterous laughter
and penis jokes.
Probably not.

The other guests are
far more somber
than my friends.

Thank fuck for my friends.

I never expected to be here.
I never thought that I would survive
long enough to be here.
I kinda hoped that
I wouldn't live long enough
to be here.
But I did.
I survived.
I survived.
I SURVIVED.

Now what the fuck do I do?

Hundred Million

There are a hundred million things I could be doing,
a hundred million dreams that I could dream.
There are a hundred million songs that I could listen to,
and a hundred million movies waiting to be watched,
with a hundred million beautiful people in them.
I could plant my feet on a hundred million different lands
or slip my eyes over a hundred million stars in the sky.
But there is nothing that I would rather do,
nothing I would rather dream,
no song I'd rather hear,
no people that I would rather see,
no place I'd rather be,
and no star that shines as brightly
as you.

Laughing by the River in the Fog

Damp and cold cling to my arms
and legs and face,
but inside I am a crackling fire by a Christmas tree,
(even though YOU'RE the one who loves Christmas)
causing steam and fog to gather close around us.
I hold you in my arms to pass the warmth,
my eyes close to yours,
I can see the smile lines
that deepen as I sing you silly songs
and whisper nonsense into your ear.
Our bond keeps us warm,
wrapped only in knit yarn and boots,
leaping over stones
and touching the small of your back with my ice-cold hand.

And that is where I keep you,
wrapped in the cold misty morning in the mountains in winter.
That is where I keep you,
laughing by the river in the fog.

Nests

If I said she was grace,
I'd be lying.
But she is grace in my eyes
with her irreverent words
and her splintered thoughts.
And who knows what,
if anything,
the world could have been
with her eyes super imposed
over mine,
or how we could have swum through the world
with our bodies and mind become one.
If only circumstances had not
intervened.
Who could know?
But I hope that
no matter where
she finds
a place to nest
she realizes that
she still has wings
etched into her shoulder blades,
and a soul tenacious
and untethered.

Now That I Have Been Saved

It's funny
that I should write love poetry now,
now that you are gone,
when before I was only able to write sad boy songs of despair
with you in my arms.
But I was broken then,
and now I have been saved,
or saved myself,
I should say.
And now with a clear mind
free from the dusty cobwebs of my anger
and sorrow
and melancholy,
I find only you
and in you I find only love.

Now that I have been saved,
I see what you truly meant
and I found how I truly felt,
and now all that's left to do is feel it.

The Pewter Chalice

I will tell you now the story of my friend Daniel Thomas, though it is a somber tale, and it brings me no pleasure to tell. I will tell you everything that I know, what I saw with my own eyes, and what grief was conveyed to me by my friend before he left this physical plane. I tell you so that you may know what lies beyond, on the edges of the oldest memory of the oldest book. I tell you so that you may be prepared for what will come.

Daniel was in Avril's Antiques and Oddities when he found The Cup. It was made of pewter, worn with age, and from Daniel's telling, was wedged between an old encyclopedia and portrait of a man that had decayed such that his visage no longer appeared human.

There was no indication then of what power The Cup held, nor did the proprietor of the curiosity shop offer any warning. If they had, perhaps it would have saved Daniel the horror he would experience. But perhaps it would have changed nothing, and all of our choices are already determined by the Gods before we are ever born. Who knows what is true? It is not my place to question.

The Cup, you see, was cast in pewter pulled from deep within the earth, and ancient beyond the reckoning of mankind, though you wouldn't know it by looking at it. By all appearances, it was a simple pewter cup, worn with age. Daniel thought that it would be a good cup to drink ale from.

After paying two dollars for The Cup, Daniel brought the pewter chalice home and placed it on his counter as he went about his day. There it sat, undisturbed, as it quickly slipped from Daniel's mind in the bustle of his everyday activity.

And, oh, how lucky it would have been for Daniel, and for myself, if it had stayed there, out of his thoughts and out of his life. But, as fate would have it, Daniel remembered about the cup in the evening two days later, poured himself a drink, and took a large swig.

Have you ever momentarily forgotten your brother's name? Or that feeling where you can't remember what street you took to get to the store? Well, Daniel, after one drink from his cup, lost an hour in the same fashion. He awoke, lying on his study floor. His head, split as if rent by God himself, reeled in the midafternoon sun, and he realized that his hands were covered in ink.

Though he searched for anything that he may have written to cause his hands to be so stained, he could find no parchment, no book that he had so written in. The thought that The Cup could have been the issue never even crossed his mind, until it was far too late. Instead he made excuses for his lost time. He was taken ill. Exhaustion. The ale had turned. And so he did what any intelligent man would do—he dumped the ale out the window, scrubbed the ink from his hands, and went to bed.

And so the entire affair drifted softly from his memory, until two weeks later, when, after a long evening in the tavern, he returned home, and poured himself one last mead in the pewter tankard to cap off his night. He sipped the sweet honey wine, his lips matted with the thick sugar, and promptly fell into a deep sleep.

Of his dream, he was unable or unwilling to tell me much. He said that he saw a dark sky, a sky filled with stars he had never seen, and planets spinning far too close to the earth. He saw streaks of light burning through the darkness above, and some great beast flying through the air. A great beast that flew like an angel but whose body was beyond comprehension.

And when he opened his mouth to scream, instead he found himself chanting, a booming voice filled with passion and dangerous intentions. And his chant was greeted by chanting in kind, many voices speaking as one. When he turned, he found himself standing before dozens of people, clad in crude animal hide, and bowing before him.

He looked down at his arms and found he had a deep scar in his wrist, a half circle filled with tight triangles meeting in the center. The scar was not new but still blood flowed freely and trickled down his arm and dripped to the earth. And as it dripped, the ground shook with wonderous purpose, and he lost himself in it until he awoke and found himself lying on his bed drenched in sweat.

But as his eyes focused in the dark, he realized that he was not only covered in sweat, but also his fresh blood, and found a fresh wound carved into his left wrist. A half circle with tight triangles meeting in the center.

This is when I entered this tale, as Daniel was a friend of mine, and I had not seen him in several weeks, which was odd as he was an old school friend, and we met regularly on Friday evenings to read poetry written by a mutual friend from our youth. After the second week of our missed engagement, I knew something must be amiss and brought it upon myself to visit my friend at his home. And, thus, I found myself at his door just as dusk was settling in one early Thursday evening.

The man that opened the door when I knocked was simply a shade of the man that I had the pleasure of reading poetry with just a month prior. His eyes were sunken and stared beyond me to something that wasn't there. He hadn't washed in several days and appeared to have worn the same set of clothing the entire time. But when he spoke, I could hear the soul of the man that I called my friend, and so I followed him into his home when he invited me in.

I found his living quarters, amazingly in retrospect, as clean as they had ever been. They did not reflect the wretchedness that had befallen my friend, and so I sat myself on his lounging chair as he made a pot of tea for the two of us to share.

Upon his return, I asked if he had fallen ill, for his skin had taken on a pallor that was uncharacteristic of his normally rosy demeanor. He told me that he had not slept in many days and went on to tell me the tale which I have now passed on to you.

Needless to say, I did not believe a word of it. How could I? I, a man of science and facts, will not be persuaded by the comings and goings of fever dreams. And I told Daniel as much, and though he begged and pleaded and showed me the scar on his wrist, I would not be swayed in my belief that the entire thing was in his mind. I told him that he must have taken ill and that I would fetch the doctor to come and give him the medicine he would need to break the fever that so clearly gripped his body.

And so it was that I returned the next morning with the doctor and found my friend passed out on the floor of his study, his face in the rug and his hands smudged with ink. The doctor and I pulled him to his feet and walked him to his bedroom, though he was in such a daze that he hardly recognized the hands under his shoulders holding him up. When we laid him in bed, however, his eyes opened, and he stared directly at me and, in as lucid of a voice as ever, said "The book! Find the book! Destroy it!" He was, then, overcome once again by the daze in which we had found him.

I left the doctor, then, to his study of my friend's health and ventured to my friend's office to see if I could locate whatever book Daniel was raving about in his fever. But while I searched his desk, and his bookshelves, and his living area, I could find no book besides the books of literature that my friend frequented.

I returned, after my fruitless search, to the doctor who said that my friend was gripped by fever and needed rest to burn the disease from his body. He provided a concoction that he claimed would help my friend sleep, poured it down his throat, and followed it with a drink of water from the pewter tankard, which was sitting beside Daniel's bed.

The same pewter tankard, of course, which he had drunk from to start this whole ordeal. Not that any of us knew.

I left my friend then as he began to doze, with a promise that I would return the next night to make sure that he was okay and that his fever had not worsened. And so, after closing the curtains to pitch his room into darkness, I left his home. I wonder sometimes if I could have prevented what was to come had I stayed instead of returning to my office, but it does not do to dwell on what could have been.

Regardless, I returned the next day and found the door to my friend's home sitting slightly ajar. When I knocked upon it, it creaked open softly, and I called "Hello?" and was greeted with only silence. "Hello! Daniel? Are you well?" I shouted again and again heard no reply. But this time, I was able to hear footsteps and so I stepped inside my friend's home to make sure that he was okay.

When I entered his living chamber, I saw him standing with his back to me, dazedly staring forward.

"There you are, Daniel," I said. "I called and knocked, but you did not reply. How are you feeling this evening?"

As I spoke, he turned around to look at me, and I saw in that dim light that once again his hands had ink on them, though this time they were truly covered. And so I walked to his kitchen and brought a towel back to help clean him.

It was then, as I approached him in the growing twilight, that I saw behind him there was the body of a man lying on the wooden floor, his head split in two and his life pooling around him. And I saw then that my friend's hands were not covered in ink.

I recoiled, but then my friend spoke to me and reached out his coated hands and touched my arm, and when he spoke, I could hear the fear trickling from his voice.

"My friend, please. Please, this was not me. I did not harm this man. It was some creature, some foul beast, let loose in my home. You have to believe me. You have to help me. Please."

I still don't know why I helped him then, when I should have ran to the nearest constable and washed my hands of the entire thing. I do not know if it was loyalty, my own good nature, or if some foul thing used his voice to curse me into servitude. Whatever the reason, I handed my friend the towel and then walked over to the body and picked up the arms.

Up close, I could tell the body was of a young man, maybe in his twenties. I did not know him, God bless, and his clothes identified him as someone who slept on the streets, and as sad as I am to admit, I breathed a sigh of relief at that because it was less likely that anyone would come looking for him.

I helped my friend carry the body down his cellar stairs and into the damp dirt room beneath his house. And there we dug for what must have been hours, me using the shovel in the back of the cellar and him using a gardening trowel to churn up the dirt. We laid the body to rest there and covered it with dirt, then busied ourselves around the freshly dug grave until you could not tell that it was any different from the rest of the foundation. It sickens me now to remember the sharp sound of that shovel digging into the freshly churned dirt as I laid a body to rest without a proper burial.

And so, exhausted, as it was well past midnight, both he and I walked back into his living quarters, covered in dirt and the remains of the poor soul we had just interred. I resolved that I would stay the night, as walking home this late covered in dirt would arouse suspicion, and my friend poured us a night cap to help us sleep after our dark task.

He returned after a time with a brandy for each of us, his in glass and mine in the pewter tankard that I had seen by his bedside the night before. My hands were shaking, and my mind was craving a drink, so I grabbed the cup like a tether and raised it to my lips.

As it brushed my lips, I had a brief flash of something great and ethereal. I was standing in a field and a beast stood in front of me, over four men tall, and so imposing it blotted out the purple sky.

I recoiled then and threw the cup from my hands, my heart beating out of my chest, and it was then that I finally believed the stories that my friend had told me just days before. I saw him then for what he was, an addict living on what he saw on the other side. I saw the dirt in my fingernails and the sick, sallow skin around the scar on Daniel's wrist, and it was all too much for me and I passed out right there in his living room.

I don't know how long I slumbered, but when I awoke, I found that my friend had begun lighting candles around the living room, great sticks of white wax illuminating the darkness of the night. Was it still night, or was it night again? I knew not, but I watched my friend continue to light candles, unbeknownst that I had awoken.

As he finished his ritualistic lighting of the candles, he walked slowly to the study, and it was then that I discovered why we were unable to find the book while we were in our right mind. I watched as Daniel pulled aside a loose brick from his wall and pulled a beat-up leather tome from inside, ink staining the cover. He reverently returned the brick to its place and walked over to me.

And though I feigned sleep, my friend, or what was left of him, picked me up with a strength I had never seen in him before, and set me on my feet. I was so startled that I didn't even pretend to be asleep and stood facing the empty husk that used to be Daniel Thomas.

He smiled at me and gestured to the candles. "You have seen, now. You know why. You are one with us." And as he spoke, he showed me the book, filled with crude lines of a vicious old language that I had never seen before. But even so, I could read it. I could read it as if it was a memory buried in my mind, and I think that any man that walks this earth would be able to read those words for they were planted there long before our grandparents' grandparents were born.

And what they spoke of…a great darkness, a reign of blood, the great awakening. Fear gripped me then, and my legs stuck to the ground as if by some great force. I could do nothing as Daniel took the book back and walked toward the many candles that cast ghostly shadows across the room.

He began speaking, and now his voice had lost any proof that this was ever my friend Daniel. He spoke with a commanding, booming voice, thick with all the fear and hatred of the world, the words oozing from his lips and dripping to the floor. As he spoke, he used the blade of a knife to carve deep, deep into the muscle of his arm, and dripped the blood in a half circle on the ground, in the opposite direction of the scar on his arm.

The blood began to glow, a sickly violet color, and as the half circle was completed, I felt a rush of wind, and the candles went out. There, cast in darkness, I saw the purple sky that I had seen in my vision, and limbs, if you can call them limbs, but I have no other words to describe the writhing mass that stood before me. And they reached out, slowly to our world, slowly creeping through the prison that had kept them for eons. They extended toward my old friend's outstretched arm and touched. And when they did, I felt reality shatter around me.

Then, and only then, could I find the courage to move.

I ran forward, grabbing a candelabrum as I went, the burnt wax clattering to the floorboards. Daniel was facing the horror on the other side of reality and was still chanting in his commanding voice, and he never saw me. It is probably for the best, for I don't know if I could have brought the heavy brass candle holder across his head had I seen the eyes of my old friend. But as I did not, I brought it down again and again and again.

There was a scream then. A horrible, curdled scream that ripped through my head and sent me to my knees. The great beast reached out and wrapped a limb around Daniel's arm but was pitched back by some unearthly force, and I felt reality crash back in around me and the beast jerked away, taking my friend Daniel's arm with it. My friend stood for a moment, and then, armless, blood pouring down his side, fell to the ground and did not draw another breath.

At last, everything was quiet, and I knelt alone covered in the remains of my friend, who lay beside me with his head crushed in and his arm ripped off, and there I succumbed to blackness for the second time that night. Which is where they found me the next morning, lying on the floor of my friends' home, covered in his blood clutching a candle stick in my hand.

I do not know why they found his body buried in the cellar. I do not know why they never found the body of the street urchin that Daniel had killed earlier that day, nor why there was never any sign of the book again. But I do know that they never found my friend's left arm, and I know that they never will, and I would be willing to guess that the book is hidden behind a loose brick in his study. Somehow... Somehow, I know.

But I didn't do what they said that I did! I did not kill my friend in anger. I did not kill my friend out of jealousy or spite. I did it of love. I did it to free him of the power that held him, and I did it to save us all.

I am not mad. I know what I saw, but I understand that most will not believe me. I didn't believe my friend until it was far too late. But I tell you these things... I tell you all so that one of you may listen and may heed my warning before I am dragged off to the stocks. Somewhere out there, The Cup is still sitting, waiting for another to drink from it and learn the secrets of the Old Gods. Somewhere out there is a book that opens a door somewhere far worse than hell. And I hope on the day that some poor soul finds it, there is someone as strong as me there to do what must be done!

For the Old Gods are still there. And my god! They are so hungry.

Once Again

I know that your life,
as with mine,
is about finding yourself
and where you want to be in the world.
But I hope one day
you find that the place you want to be
in the world,
is reflected in my eyes
once again.

The Law of Conservation of Mass

The law of conversation of mass
tells us that our bodies
and souls,
while constantly changing,
leave the old pieces of ourselves to the universe,
to mix with the stardust
and the early morning dew.
None of us ever really go away.
There are pieces of my youth
in every drop of rain
that falls in the late fall Seattle showers,
and there are pieces of your beauty
in the sunflowers poking from the earth.
And that means,
somewhere out there among the stars and the morning sky,
there are pieces of ourselves
that are still entwined,
and will still be there
long after my lips
drift from the memory of your neck.

Six Months Sober—Essay

On Monday, October 28, I will have been sober for six months. Given the nature of this milestone for me, I've been extremely reflective about all the changes I've made. To be fair, most of those changes kicked in three months ago, but hey…that's still within the last six months, so deal with it. Honestly, with the changes I've made to my life, my outlook, my daily routine, I feel like a completely different person. In the last six months, I have done the following:

- started meditating twenty to thirty minutes a day;
- started being more proactive of eating along my diet (seriously, gut health really does impact mental health);
- started going to the gym five days a week and learning how to make the most impact in my workouts;
- did thirty pull ups in the morning and thirty more in the evening;
- gained twelve pounds, related to the above, all muscle weight;
- changed the medication regimen that I'm on to help with anxiety and not just depression;
- started doing yoga, both in classes and at home (trying to build up a better knowledge base of poses, etc., so I don't need to watch everyone around me);
- started writing more—five chapters in an autobiographical book, three chapters in a novel I'm working on, three short ghost stories, multiple lengthy self-reflective Facebook posts (*hey, a lot of these ended up in this book!*);
- started reading self-help books—basically getting the information directly from the experts on how to help myself;
- started approaching my therapy sessions with more intention;

- gone from seeing my therapist twice a week (they want you to talk to a therapist more often after you try killing yourself for some reason) to once every other week, because I've taken on more of my self-discovery and reflection on my own;
- stopped drinking, obviously;
- started drinking a *lot* more water (seriously, it's pretty much all I drink now);
- worked on healing relationships with friends and family members, including some very difficult conversations;
- became incredibly close with my brother Alex and his wife Deanna for the first time in my life (not that we ever had problems, we just were both more independent and didn't do much to connect before);
- worked on skills I've wanted to work on for a while—such as video editing;
- kept my living space clean to help my focus;
- started writing music (emphasis on the *started*, but still);
- really viewed myself for what I was, including faults and strengths so that I could be better;
- started healing trauma so that I could start thriving and not just surviving;
- started listening to therapy podcasts and following therapy Instagram accounts;
- went to the dermatologist and had my skin tabs removed and got medicated treatment for my acne (what can I say, I'm a little vain and figure if I'm improving my inside, I can also improve my outside and also, they checked me for skin cancer which runs in my family, so it was a win-win);
- improved my sleep, and I basically sleep through the night every night, which has been a struggle for me for *years*;
- stopped blaming others for how I feel and started being less emotionally reactive;
- started listening to myself—both my wants and my needs, and started setting boundaries accordingly;

- started leaving my apartment more often on my days off, even if it's just to go to a café for a bit (*this did not age well in 2020*);
- stopped going to parties and large gatherings or listening to myself when I get anxious because of them and choose to leave early;
- listened more actively—whether if it's with a friend talking about a problem or in a meeting;
- started being more expressive with how I feel in a healthy way;
- drank *way* less caffeine (I went from drinking four or five cups of coffee a day to a cup or two of tea, normally green tea), which in turn, has helped me feel *way* less anxious every day;
- ate a lot of rice now (that's not really here or there, but I figured I'd mention it);
- started appreciating the support that my friends and family give me;
- started living more in the moment and experiencing what is around me; and
- started being happy that I'm alive.

There's probably a bunch of other stuff that I'm not remembering right now, so this covers all of those.

Now, don't get me wrong. I'm not *literally* a different person. I still love noir films, comic books, playing board and tabletop games, Luna, video games, and Netflix. The difference is that I'm not just doing those things. I'm also doing the things that my body *needs* and not just running around trying to do things that give my body a high. I've learned to appreciate the difference between being mentally healthy and happy that I don't need to be "happy" constantly. That it's okay to feel bad sometimes, as long as I don't let myself slide into it and make a home in that bad feeling. I've learned that I can process my feelings, take care of myself, and do the things that I love.

Basically, I've learned how to be a human. And I'm so happy for it.

So here's to six months sober. And self-growth. And to many, many more years of both.

Do You Know How Important You Are?

Do you realize how important
I find you?
How important every single
one of your performances are,
sitting in a dingy bar
and being enveloped in your voice?
How important each night is—
falling asleep next to you,
and waking up to the sounds of your
night terrors and telling you
it's going to be okay,
it's going to be okay.
I have you in my arms and I won't
let your mind carry you away again?
Do you realize how often
you consume my mind,
and carry me away to
a small hill
with you lying next to me
in the grass
with books above our faces?
Do you feel how the
strings from your heart
reach out and wrap around mine—
a harp I play
every time I say your name
and create music—
the most important song that I have ever played.

Do you know how important you are?

Exultation

I would have my passion
turn to wild exultation,
to have my fingers dance upon your skin
instead of over these cold keys,
to have my words slide from my lips
to your ears
to your mouth
to your belly
to wherever they trail next.
I would have my breath
draw bumps on your breasts,
and my nails track valleys down your legs.
But instead I will continue to write these worlds
and only kiss your lips in my mind.

Grammy

When I was young,
for a time,
I was shorter than
my Grammy
and looked up to her
with my baby eyes
and cherub cheeks
as she picked cookies and glasses
from the tall shelves that I couldn't reach.

Well, I didn't stay
shorter than her for long,
but to this day,
as I help her get plates and
serving trays from the highest shelf
tucked back in the corner,
I still look up to her.
I still find
my heart
and my mind
and my love
built on the foundation
of her hands
and Saturday morning yard sales
on warm spring weekends.

Colby Ave

My Memere
was the type of woman
that told everyone to call
her Memere.
It didn't matter who you were,
if anyone in her family cared for you
there was a safe space for you in her home,
and a place set at the table.
There were gifts under the tree,
and a bed you could sleep on
no matter what your life
had turned into.

My Pepere
was the type of man
who kept a garden
and offered you
fresh vegetables for your salad,
or to take a bite from a tomato
that tasted like yesterday.
His toolshed
was the best spot to hide
when you were hiding from
the seeker as the sun
was going down on soft
Massachusetts summer days.

Their house was a place for
family,
for safety,
where chivalry still thrived

and laughter was the only
currency you needed
every Wednesday, Thursday, and Friday.
It was pool in the summer,
and sledding down hills
that were definitely not safe to sled down
in the snow.

It has been many years now
since my cousins and I
ran rough shod
over the grass on that ave in Worcester.
My feet no longer
find purchase on those seven hills,
and my eyes haven't seen the sunset
of an east coast evening
in many years.
But in my heart
every day is a day on Colby Ave,
and my Memere and Pepere
live on forever
drinking tea
together
on the plastic tablecloth
in their dining room.

To Grandmother's House I Go

My grandmother has lived in
five different houses
that I remember.
I'm sure she's lived in more than
just those, though.
The house has changed,
different color siding,
different shapes,
different states...
some where I slept in the basement with my father,
some I slept in spare bedrooms,
and some I never slept in at all.

But no matter what house,
no matter what color
or state
or even how long she lived there,
I was always welcome.
And sometimes,
when I felt like I had nowhere else to go,
that invitation
made all the difference
in the world.

Save Me in Singapore—Essay

I've been back in Seattle for a day, mostly caught up on sleep and have my body back on something like a normal schedule. I've been petting my cat a lot (she was very upset that I left her like that) and appreciating the beauty in Seattle as well. Also, it's been great to be at an actual gym again and not the tiny hotel gym (though it is sad that I don't have an awesome pool to swim in).

Singapore was absolutely amazing. Everyone was super nice, the food was amazing, and it was eye-opening to be in a place that is not so Western focused. It was different than anything that I was used to, and that taught me a lot about myself. Getting to partake in a completely different culture is an experience that I think everyone should have.

Also, if you get the chance to travel for work, do it. It was amazing to get to swim every night before bed, the view was amazing, and don't even get me started on how great it is to have your food comped. I know that I am extremely lucky and privileged to have this experience, but I wouldn't trade it for the world.

While I was away, I continued on my journey of self-discovery and understanding. If anything, I doubled down on it because I didn't have quite as much to distract me, especially on the plane. A seventeen-hour flight is no joke. I read books about how to better keep myself in a positive mindset, how to better handle chemical dependencies (including caffeine, which I have also cut back tremendously on), but most importantly on relationships—focusing on codependency and attachment styles in relationships. The entire experience—reading, having time to myself, meditating twice a day, swimming—has shown me a lot. I've been listening to myself more, being honest with myself about my mistakes, coming up with strategies to not repeat those mistakes and fix my mindset. I've been arming myself with information so that I can better communicate, care for people, and live the best life that I can.

The fact of the matter is that for a long, long time now (years? decades? my entire life?), I've been incredibly depressed. I've never felt particularly balanced, and because of that, I've worked on guarding myself, building up extreme walls to keep people out and putting on a face that everything is okay. I've never been able to communicate how I was feeling to others in a way that made me feel comfortable. It was either I never talked, or I exploded with my emotions. I didn't appropriately take care of them. Sure, when things would get really bad, I'd go to therapy but only once the problem had already boiled over. And once I was there, I would stop going as soon as I felt better…never really fixing anything, never making the changes that I needed to make. I continued drinking too much to help myself feel better in the moment, despite the fact that it would make things far worse for me and those around me. I'd work too much, take on too many things, not focus on things I cared about, and burn myself out. I shut people away, kept myself distant from people. I took anyone's criticism of my choices as a personal attack against me, and not as the indicator of care that it was, that they were looking for me to make changes for the better. Instead, I argued, disbelieved, and never put the appropriate work into myself. I was never honest with myself.

And, of course, this has always spilled into damaging my relationships.

For those of you familiar with attachment styles, I am the wonderful anxious-avoidant. I keep my partners at arm's length, but once they get close, I latch on too hard. Which, of course, creates a wonderful cycle of self-abuse and relationship estrangement. It wasn't fair to them, and it wasn't fair to me. For everyone that I've hurt due to this, I'm sorry. It never had anything to do with you specifically, but with the depression in my head that I left unchecked, the issues that I never resolved, only tried hiding under a rug. If it ever seemed like I hated you, or anyone, I can promise that the only person that I really hated was myself for letting myself get this way.

I realized a month and a half ago that I had three choices, really. One of them was to stay the same and watch the same thing happen again and again. The second was to break the cycle and do a lot of self-critical thinking and make the important changes that I needed to make. The third was to die. To be fair, I did at first choose the third option. But when I got to that point, when I looked over the edge, I realized (with the help of some of my closest friends and family) that I didn't really want that. That what I wanted was change, not death. And my choices to that point had only been building myself to explode, to take my own life. I used to joke it was an inevitability for me. It wasn't really a joke; I really did believe that. But now I see what I was doing, the fact that since I thought that way, since I viewed it as an inevitable ending in my life, of course it was where my life headed. And I realized that the real thing I needed to do was be honest with myself about the bad things, to process them, and let myself change and move on with my life in a valid way. In a constructive way.

And so I have. I've started meditating, which has been life changing. I've read books that really show me how my actions impact other people and how their actions have impacted me. I've realized my issues with not communicating, which is why I've been so open about everything lately. It's practice. I've started exercising regularly. Started eating better and cheating on my diet less (not weight-loss diet, health diet). I've started talking to people more often and not closing myself off but also spending more specific time with just myself so that I can listen to my needs. I don't keep myself so busy that I burn out. I don't feel the need to constantly be doing something—I've started to enjoy the quiet moments. I've started living in the moment more, which meditation has really helped me with—enjoying the time I spend and not dwelling on the past or concerning myself with the future of what might be. My therapy appointments have become a lot more focused and helpful, especially now that I've made the personal decision to grow as much as possible. I've become receptive to change. And I've cut *waaaayyyyyy* down on my caffeine intake, which has made me feel way less anxious all the time.

I've already seen the differences and can feel the change building up inside me as well. My mind has quieted in a way I never thought possible. I like myself more and can help myself when I get down. I can see past myself and into the lives of those around me better to how I impact their lives and how I can better be a part of them. I've been more focused and productive at work. My physical health has gotten a lot better, and the working out has helped me look the best I ever have as well (which is also nice for my self-esteem, even if in a vain kind of way). I enjoy being alive.

Self-care is not easy. This has been an incredibly heart-wrenching and difficult climb to get where I am. There have been times where I've fallen down, but I've pulled myself back up and climbed higher than before. I encourage everyone to take the time to really listen to yourself, care for yourself, and grow into yourself. Learn from my mistakes and grow now before you fall as deep as I did. You don't need to hit rock bottom to make a change.

Once again, I want to apologize to everyone that has been hurt by my thinking this way. I know that I am evolving into the best version of myself that I can be, that I know I can work on myself and continue to grow. I know that I'll never stop, that self-growth is a lifetime decision, and I will be continuing to do this my entire life. I'm okay with that. It's better to dedicate my life to living than it is to dedicate my life to dying.

Cacophony

She flops
and flails
and sinks
and sails
and dances
along the thin membrane
between life and love
and death and change
and finds her body burning—
one moment in despair
and the next like a comet across the dark night sky.
Everything is too much,
and not enough
all at once,
a swirling life of vertigo and saints
and cursed decks of cards.
But even then,
in the whirlwind of her own mind,
she finds the beauty
to inspire herself
to wake up each morning and say,
"Okay, I'll try again."

I Have a Record Player

I have a record player
and a couple hundred records,
and about five of them that I can't play.
They aren't scratched,
not literally, at least.
But they still have the open wounds
that I had on my ankles
that I left on myself in your wake,
and the cracked, dry skin,
caused by the pills that were supposed to keep me alive
but almost caused me to die.
I suppose the pills didn't almost cause me to die,
as if it was some kind of accident.
But the records I have,
spinning sad boy songs
about new jersey,
and the cool,
and women tied to ladders,
and smoke I tried too hard to hold...
I always tried too hard to hold.
I can't listen to these anymore,
because they skip more beats than you used to cause my heart,
and they still carry
your scent
on the memory
of Brian Fallon's words.

But What If It Was?

We sit in it as the lights slowly come up on *SKYLER and JAEL. JAEL is lying on a hospital bed, weak and riddled with cancer. They are close to death, as what happens to us all. SKYLER sits in a chair next to them, the grief of loss that has yet to happen draping over them both. SKYLER is still trying to put on a happy face for their partner in the bed.*

SKYLER

Wow, Jael! Did you know in Sweden, you don't need permission or a pass or anything to be able to camp pretty much wherever. No campground, just out in the woods in nature. I think we should go camping this summer...

JAEL

Skyler, we talked about this. But you should go.

SKYLER

But I don't want to go without you. I want you to come with me.

SKYLER sits forward and takes JAEL's hand in theirs.

So how about it. You and me, a tent, and just miles of Swedish woods. They even have the most McDonald's per capita, so we can get you a McFlurry.

JAEL

That sounds really nice, Skyler.

The two lapse into silence, both knowing that it won't be able to happen.

Look, I want you to promise me something.

SKYLER

Well, I'm not just going to blindly promise without knowing what it is first. I've made that mistake with you before.

JAEL

Please, just promise.

SKYLER

Okay, I promise. What is it?

JAEL

I just want you to promise that when I'm gone, you're still going to go to Sweden...

SKYLER

But that's not going to happen, Jael. You're going to beat this thing, you're gonna get better.

JAEL

Please, I don't want my last thoughts to be of you giving up.

SKYLER

I'm not giving up. And you're not giving up. You're a fighter, right? You just gotta keep fighting for me.

JAEL

Skyler, this...this isn't just a cold. You know what the doctors said.

SKYLER

I don't care what the doctors said! People beat this every day.

JAEL

But not this time. It's okay... I-I've come to terms with that. At this point, it would take—

SKYLER

A miracle. That's what we need! A miracle!

JAEL

Miracles don't just happen. I just don't want you to die with me. You're going to still be here. You can still go on those trips. You can still see Sweden. You'll just have to see it on your own.

SKYLER

I can't do that. I can't let you go. I need you with me to see Sweden. I need you in my life to sing songs with and tell bedtime stories and dance with. I can't do that alone. So I need a miracle.

Enter MAXXAMERICLE. He is a bustle of energy, dressed in a white lab coat and wearing a stethoscope around his neck. He speaks with an over-the-top accent and has the energy of a rhinoceros on cocaine.

MAXXAMERICLE

Ahh, so you must be the patient, eh? Terrible, terrible thing that. Cancer. Awful. Giant crabs in the sky, no one needs that, am I right? You're here on earth. Don't need any giant crabs riddling your body, eh?

JAEL

I'm...sorry, Doctor? Could you give us just a minute? We need a moment. We're saying our goodbyes.

MAXXAMERICLE

Goodbyes, hellos, what's the difference? You end up waving either way. Not like the wave at the ocean, mind you, but with your hand.

Now, what did I come in here for, sorry, lost my train of thought. Oh yes, cancer! You have cancer!

JAEL

Yes, Doctor, that's why we were saying our goodbyes.

MAXXAMERICLE

But that's why I'm here. You can stop saying your goodbyes because you have the exact qualifications that I'm looking for, Jael, to be the first human test subject for my brilliant new cancer drug! I've been developing it for the last four years, and it has completely removed the cancer from every one of the rats that I've tested it on! It's very experimental, mind you, but I know that it will cure you. It is, simply put, a miracle.

JAEL

I don't know.

SKYLER

Honey, please, like he said, it's a miracle. It's exactly what we need. If there's a chance, any chance, that this could help you, we need to try.

JAEL

I guess... Doctor, what are the side effects?

MAXXAMERICLE

Side effects? I come in here saying that I can cure cancer and you're worried about an upset tummy? Side effects! Pah. Some of the rats saw a decrease in their sex drive, but just have your partner here give you a little extra jiggle jiggle and you'll be fine. Maybe some headaches or something else. But nothing much. And may I remind you, I am offering to save your *fucking* life. Do the side effects outweigh that?

JAEL

I guess not. I... Well, what do I have to lose, right? Okay. Okay, I'll do it.

MAXXAMERICLE

Of course you will!

MAXXAMERICLE suddenly lunges forward and pokes JAEL with a needle.

JAEL

Ow! How about a little warning?

MAXXAMERICLE

I'm sorry. The cure only works with the element of surprise. It has to sneak up on the cancer you see.

SKYLER

How long will it take for us to know if it worked?

JAEL

We don't have long to wait. The other doctors only gave me another couple days...

MAXXAMERICLE

Oh, no worries, the medication takes effect almost immediately. See, I can see the color coming back into your face already!

SKYLER

You do look a lot better. How... How do you feel?

JAEL

I feel... I feel good! I feel better than I have in years, Skyler!

JAEL gets up, full of energy and alive. JAEL and SKYLER embrace, both overcome by excitement and love.

I can't believe this! This is... This is incredible. Thank you, thank you, Doctor... I'm sorry. I didn't even get your name. I owe you my life, and I never even got your name.

MAXXIMERICLE

Oh, you can just call me Max. I'm so glad to see that this is another rousing success! Well, I will leave you two to saying your goodbyes or hellos or whatever it is you feel like. Would you like me to put a sock on the door, perhaps?

JAEL and SKYLER hardly listen, and MAXXIMERICLE wasn't looking for a response. He delivers the line as he's already walking out of the room.

SKYLER

Jael. Jael, I love you so much. This is amazing. Now we can both go to Sweden, and I can hold you every night and whisper stories into your ear. Jael, you are the most amazing person I've ever met.

JAEL

Skyler... I love you. I love you more than anything. Thank you for standing by me through all of this. I can't wait to spend every second of the rest of my life with you. To watch you grow old, with gray hair. To go swimming in the ocean. And to... And to dance. Skyler, I just want to dance with you. Right now! Come here!

JAEL grabs SKYLER into a close embrace, and the two start swaying, softly dancing in the room alone in silence.

SKYLER

I think we should sell the house, Jael. I think we should sell it, and I'll quit my job, and we should just go travelling. Just you and me. Will you see the world with me?

JAEL

That sounds amazing, Skyler. Let's get a Winnebago and just drive. I don't want to waste another second of my life.

The two sway in love. Beat.

SKYLER

I never noticed how much I loved the smell of your hair before. I could stay in this moment forever.

JAEL

I could, too. I could spend every minute of forever just here swaying in your arms, so close to you. But, Skyler, you know this isn't what happened.

SKYLER

I know, love, I know. But what if it was? What if it was?

The two continue to sway softly as the lights go down.

Hotel Bed

There has never been anything
as lovely as your face,
and shoulders,
and tattoos
bathed in dim lamplight
lying next to me on this hotel bed.

I Remember

I remember waking up
in the middle of the night
because you were screaming in your sleep
again.
I remember holding you
until you were able to calm down,
remember turning the lights on so that you would know that
there wasn't a murderer in the house,
remember telling you everything was going to be okay,
be okay,
be okay.
I remember holding you
in the dark,
because the light was too much
for the manic episode that you felt building.
I remember finding the soft music that would help you
relax,
the fast music that would pick you up,
and "My Shiny Teeth and Me" to make you laugh.
I remember you,
every wrinkle, every moment of sadness,
every scent,
every strand of long hair shed on the
bed, couch, floor,
everywhere.

I remember you.

I Would

I would breathe you in,
consume you,
taste you,
let you linger on my tongue
as it gropes blindly over your body
beneath mine.

I would hold you,
your skin against mine,
my fingers in your hair,
my eyes watching my body
reflected in yours.

I would have us become one,
our breath as one,
our hands as one,
your voice in my ear,
your mind echoing in mine.

And I would have us,
tired and spent and connected,
so connected,
lay in the quiet of our bed
and listen to nothing but your
heartbeat under my ear.

Eriksgiving—Essay

As part of the changes I've been making in my life and realizations about myself, I have made an important decision: this year will be my last Eriksgiving.

Eriksgiving (my thanksgiving/birthday celebration where I make a huge Thanksgiving dinner) has always been a day of excess for me. Excessive drinking and overeating—indulging myself to the point of delusion and becoming wholly selfish.

I've had a lot of fun with them and have good memories...but I also have a lot of bad memories of the person that I became during them and the choices I made. The choice to drink to the point that I couldn't stand, and the choice to feel victimized if everything didn't go exactly how I wanted it to. The choice to let the anxiety of it get to me and ruin the time I had.

So this year's, keeping in line with my current priorities, will be a sober Eriksgiving called Escape from Eriksgiving, where I will design an Erik-themed escape room. It seems a fitting end to the series, so that I can end them on a high note, at least.

It's a mark to end an era where I was someone I haven't liked being. Parties started filling me with anxiety a while ago, but I wasn't listening to myself and how I felt around them. Instead I blamed that anxiety on other things, and then drank so that I wouldn't feel the anxiety anymore (of course, it doesn't actually work that way). And I've been doing that for years now. But I'm finally correcting it. I'm finally listening to myself and making the changes that I need to for my mental and physical health. I'm becoming the best me.

And I can't be the best me at Eriksgiving.

Last Christmas (Not the Wham Song)

Last Christmas,
I decorated a full tree
with you
and hung garland,
and a gingerbread man was
hanging on the door.

This, even though I hated Christmas,
but I knew that it made you happy.

Last Christmas,
we had a party,
and made mulled wine
and bought way too much sandwich meat
and cheese.
It was the best Christmas party,
I have ever been to.

This, even though I hated Christmas,
but I wanted to make you happy.

Last Christmas,
I made us both
hot chocolate and poured in
Bailey's so that
we could stay warm while
we walked around the neighborhood
looking at the Christmas lights
hanging on the houses

that we knew we could never afford,
but that we would have loved to decorate ourselves.
And I would have
bought as many decorations to run along
the frame of the house
and filled the yard with animatronic reindeer
and inflatable Santa Clauses
and would have found the biggest Christmas tree you've ever seen
to sit directly in the living room window.

This, even though I hated Christmas,
but I wanted to make you smile.

Last Christmas,
I bought you tools
to make the music that
you heard in your heart and soul,
because I wanted to hear it, too.
I made us breakfast,
and we spent the day together
making new traditions,
and listening to records
and drinking cocoa.

Last Christmas,
you made me love Christmas.

I Used To

I used to write at night
long after I should have been asleep,
normally with a glass of whiskey
and probably some caffeine.
All of my poetry was sad then
because I knew nothing but loneliness, exhaustion,
and a drunken state I had confused
with bliss.

I used to sit inside with the curtains drawn,
playing video games
or mindlessly watching some TV
show that I can't even recall.
My mind was purposefully vacant,
and I would kill any braincell that tried to remind
me of the things that were wrong.
Killed with either alcohol
or mind-numbing distraction.

I used to cheat on the diet
my doctor told me I needed to follow
so that my stomach wouldn't feel like it was about to
crawl out of my rib cage.
And,
sure enough,
then my stomach would feel like it was
about to crawl out of my ribcage.
But I just wanted to feel "normal."

I used to stay out late,
I used to self-medicate,

I used to drink way too much coffee,
I used to not take my medication,
I used to only listen to sad songs,
I used to take you for granted.

I used to.
But not anymore.

Communication Part 1—Essay

Part of my current growth has been a focus on understanding how I interact in relationships. I've read a lot of books on codependency, love languages, love styles, sexuality in relationships…whatever I've been able to get my hands on. It's been incredibly eye-opening to see the way that I feel and react in relationships, why I feel certain ways and react certain ways, things I did wrong, etc.

I think my biggest breakdown in relationships has always been communication. Listening, of course, is a thing many of us struggle with. I have a tendency to want to fix things. I listen to a problem, and immediately, I just start coming up with a fix. "Do this" or "Don't do that" were almost always the first things out of my mouth after listening to someone's problems. But what most people are looking for when they talk is to be heard. They probably already know what they "should do" or avoid in the future; they're just looking for someone to listen to the problem. And giving notes and trying to "fix" the problem is likely to make them feel unheard, or even feel put down, as if you thought they couldn't fix their own problem. And there's no one who is looking to be put down.

Another aspect of that is active listening. My biggest problem was always being so caught up in my own head and trying to keep myself distracted. So I would listen, but I was listening while dwelling on how crappy I felt, or while playing a video game so that I didn't recognize how crappy I felt. I can definitely see where that wouldn't make anyone feel heard. Eye contact is so important in active listening for making someone feel heard. A great tip, as well, is to repeat things back to someone, not word for word but such as "I can definitely see where the action taken by your coworker would make you feel XYZ." This does a few things—it lets the person know you're listening, as well as making sure you actually understand them and aren't assuming to know what they mean. It'll put you on the same page and avoid any awkwardness in the future.

But the other way I've always fallen apart with communication is expressing what I need. I've never been good with this. Especially with everything in my life, I've never had much that could *take* from me. Most of my life has been giving people things—support, time, work, whatever it is that's needed in the situation. There was very little in my life that would help remove things *from* me. And after a while, I internalized so much of that. I'm sure a lot of my friends have noticed that I'll listen to someone talk about their problems until they're blue in the face but would rarely go on about my own issues.

Another aspect of that was also that I often didn't *know* what I needed or how I felt. I spent so much time trying to cover up my depression or anger that I almost wanted to believe myself when I told everyone that I was fine. So I didn't ever talk about what I needed, or set any boundaries, because I didn't *know* what I needed or wanted. Or maybe more I didn't want to think about what I needed. Either way.

It ties into why I drank. It was one of the only times that I would force my walls down enough to feel what I was feeling. To break down and cry if I needed to. But, of course, since I was drunk, those things wouldn't come out well. Whether it was to someone else or to myself, the way those pent-up emotions would leak out was like sewage—raw emotion, depression, and confusion. Which, of course, made me want to communicate less because I was afraid of what would come out.

But of course, then I'd feel my boundaries get crossed and get upset when the other person had no way to know that there even was a boundary. And of course, that would make me feel worse when I crossed a boundary of theirs. If they wouldn't respect mine, why would they expect me to respect theirs? The difference, of course, is that I knew theirs, they didn't know mine.

Communication is the number 1 thing that I'm working on now. I'm working to listen and be more present in all my relationships. I'm working to be more specific in my boundaries and letting people know when they're approaching them. It's hard. It's awkward. It's taking time. But I'm working on it so that I can fix these problems that I've had for years. And I know all of my relationships are going to benefit from it.

I'd recommend anyone—whether you're in a relationship or just want to be in one—to read books about them. Not books on how to manipulate relationships. Those books are depressing and borderline violent. I mean books about the psychology. It'll help you see patterns you have that may hurt your partner. It'll let you put words to things your partner does that hurt you. It'll help you realize those things your partner does aren't designed to hurt you and are just because they have learned patterns in their lives as well. It'll just help. And you'll find your relationships grow because of reading and learning and growing.

Anyway, thanks for coming to my ErikTalk.

Communication 2: This Time It's (More) Personal—Essay

I've mentioned before that one of my biggest issues in relationships has always been communication, which is why I'm working so hard on it lately. I've been focused on being more present, which allows me to be a more active listener and working harder to talk about the things that I'm feeling/dealing with in my life. Today, I realized part of the reason that I've always been so bad at communicating is that... I honestly didn't know *why* I was feeling that way.

When you don't know why you feel a certain way or don't know the words to help you express them, you feel cut off from everyone else. It feels like communicating is useless because the other person won't be able to walk away with understanding. So instead, I always just shut myself off. I learned the word for that today—*stonewalling*. It's about being so anxious about communicating that you literally shut down and can't communicate. The best way to counteract this issue is to walk away from the situation for about twenty minutes, do something you like such as going for a walk or meditating, and then return to the conversation. But because I didn't recognize this about myself, I would just shut down and not be able to communicate until I just started festering and then felt angry and miserable about the world. And when you feel that way, you look for something to explain it that you'll understand, which is usually an outside person close to you.

It's easy when you're feeling like that to then blame another person. Either for how you feel or for not understanding how you feel, which in turn makes you feel more isolated than before. But it's not on the other person to have to decipher what you're feeling. It's not up to them to communicate it to you (unless it's a therapist, but even then, the therapist can only help with what you tell them). So take the time to learn about yourself. Read books about relationships to figure out why you're reacting to different things or even what it is that you're reacting to. It's easy to get so caught up in reacting to relationships that you don't actually pay attention to what it is that you're reacting to. Go to therapy so that you can have an outside person help you decipher what's going on in your mind.

Learning how to better communicate will help you in so many ways. It can help you express healthy boundaries and make room in your relationship for what you need to feel valued. It will help you listen and not just simply react. It will help you stop making excuses and take responsibility for the breakdown in communication so that you can reexamine what the issue is and then figure out how to resolve it with your partner.

Every day I'm learning and seeing patterns that I've had for a long time. And every day I'm finding healthier ways to approach these issues and grow as a better person. I know whatever the future holds I will be the best person that I can and won't continue to repeat the mistakes that I've made.

Thanks for coming to my ErikTalk.

Humarock

I remember sitting on your grandmother's dock,
on the gully side
of the Atlantic Ocean,
the water too cold for us to
want to jump in.
I remember the water was so calm,
with only the gentle splash of the wake
of the boats driving past.

I wonder if you still sit there without me.
I'm sure you do.
I mean,
you had been doing it long before I came into your life,
so you're probably still doing it now.
I wonder if anyone takes your picture now,
like I did,
trying my best to capture all of you
the way that I see you.
I wonder if they see you the same.

I don't have a dock to sit on.
At least,
not on the waterfront
of eastern Massachusetts.
But sometimes, I look at a map
and am reminded that all oceans
are connected in one way or another,
and I dream.
I dream.

I am floating in the Pacific now,
gently drifted by the soft swells,
slowly,
slowly
floating further from land.
And I wonder,
if I float here long enough,
will the ocean bring me where I want to go?
Will I one day
float serenely
into the gully side
of the Atlantic Ocean
in Humarock?
And would I find you sitting there,
with your feet hanging off
the dock,
the water too cold for you to want to jump in?

Ocean Eyes

Your eyes are the ocean
behind your grandmother's house,
but not nearly as cold.
No,
I could float in them for hours,
whiling away my days
with my feet hanging off the dock,
taking pictures of you in your floppy hat
and one-piece bathing suit.
I could hold my breath and
sink below the surface,
crystal clear and filled with things unseen on this earth,
and live my life among the floating
driftwood dreams
of your mind.

The Monk Alone

Brother McCauley of the Augustinian order had been newly accepted to the Monastery of Good Hope. He had, in fact, only been living in the monastery for a week when he heard the scratch, scratch, scratch of fingernails on the heavy wooden door of the prayer room. Apprehensively, but with square shoulders and resolve in his heart, Brother McCauley reached forward and drew back the old, heavy wooden door. With a creak, the door pulled back to reveal…

Nothing.

There was nothing, and no one on the other side of the door. Only the empty prayer room cast deep in the shadows of the growing dusk.

"Hello?" he called. But he was greeted by only silence.

When he asked one of his brothers, Brother William, who had lived in the monastery for several years already, about the door to the prayer room, he was told not to worry about any noises heard about the old halls.

"The monastery is old," said William. "Of course there will be strange noises. Could not the building be settling? Or perhaps a draft could slide through a gap in the old stone walls. If the sounds of our old building bother you, perhaps the order is not right for you."

"Oh no, of course it doesn't bother me," Brother McCauley lied. "I was simply curious."

And that was the last time that Brother McCauley talked about it to any other members of the order for fear of any questioning his commitment to his faith, his god, and his duty.

But it was not the last time that he would hear the scratch, scratch, scratch upon that same door.

Just two days later, in fact, while he was carrying a tome from the library to his chamber, he heard the faint noise again. He paused his steps and listened, and as true as you can hear my voice, he could hear the unmistakable sound of fingernails scratching upon wood.

The hair on the back of his neck bristled at the sound, his resolve faltered but for a moment. But resolved or not, he set down the tome on a small table, set the candle he was using to light his path next to it, reached forward, and opened the door.

Once more, he was greeted with stillness in the chamber, though that evening the shadows were longer as the sun was soon to set. Brother McCauley stepped forward into the room, looking for any source of the noise. He felt no breeze and could not hear any creaking of a settling building.

"Hello?" he whispered.

And though there was no wind, he would have sworn on his faith that he heard a deep moan, as if dragged from the depths of hell itself.

His resolve did not hold then. He fled quickly, slamming the door behind him, and grabbed his book and candle so quick that the candle flickered and went out as he ran through the growing darkness into the safety of his room.

For the next week, he avoided the prayer room whenever he could. He would walk out of his way to cross the monastery and would only approach the room when it was required of him for his daily prayer—always with others and always when the sun was full in the sky.

But still, the sounds nagged at him, the question of what, or who, could be making the noise, as well as the question of what his duty as a member of the order, and as a Christian man, was. And so, he searched the library for any clues as to what might be causing the sound.

In all, he read through dozens of tomes, searching for any clue, many of which held no bearing on his situation. He lost sleep, staying in the library well past sundown, burning candle after candle down to the candelabrum in his quest. The other monks observed his behavior but thought that he was simply devote in his studies of the kingdom of heaven, which, of course, was common for those new to living in a monastery such as this.

Until, on the ninth day, he found a tome—old and ragged and discolored with age—that spoke of the history of the land long before the order had resided here. Many of the stories of the land differed from those which had been recorded by the monks, scathing gaps in history, as if hidden intentionally.

The building, or rather a small portion of the building, had once been used by a violent sect of monks, with a name long since forgotten, and even less pronounceable, who committed terrible sins on this land in the name of their god. The ground upon which the modern monastery was built was used in ritualistic sacrifices of those that opposed the words of their teachings, blood spilled dirt to awaken the wrath of God. And where the prayer chamber now sat was where they kept those which they would sacrifice before they were brought to the knife.

Chilled, Brother McCauley returned the book. He looked around him, as if picturing the modest library covered in the blood of those victims from years before. He thought of the lives lost and the anger and fear which was held in the very wood of this monastery, in the very dirt beneath their feet. He could almost smell the stale scent of rot and sin in the air.

He went then not to his chambers and not to the prayer room, but to the sanctuary. It was dark, as sundown had come many hours before, so he lit a candle in the darkness, knelt before the altar, and bowed his head to pray.

It is not for me to know what he asked or what he heard in response. A man's pact with God is for him and God alone. But whatever was spoken between the two in that dark sanctuary, Brother McCauley rose with resolution, his faith brimming over. He picked up his candle, along with several others from the altar. He walked out of the sanctuary and directly to the dark, cold prayer room.

Now the scratching on the door could be heard clearly. Not one set of nails, but many, a cacophony of fearful retching, clawing at any chance of escape. But the door was heavy, and they could find no salvation.

Brother McCauley threw open the door. Still, on the other side, there was nothing but darkness. But he could hear those low, lost moans floating through the air, wails of the damned themselves.

Quietly, he closed the door behind him and immediately could hear the scratching begin anew, as if the memory of those long dead fingernails was held only by the door when it was closed fast. Now, in the darkness of the room, for there was no moon on this night, he strode to the center and set the candles in a circle, lighting each from his original candle until they were all lit. And there, in the flickering light, he saw them.

Emaciated, gnawed things—ankles, wrists, necks chained to the walls. Many had open wounds and vacant eyes staring sightlessly forward, some with eyes so sunken that he could not see the color of their iris. And those who he could were clearly blinded by the long darkness that had held them. There, by the door, he could see several of these broken figures, clawing lifelessly at the door, their gnarled fingernails splintering from their fingers, spectral blood matted their hands and dripped down their arms.

And the moans. The moans became almost too much to bear. Wails of long dead lungs, mildew voices crying forth for salvation! But no answer was there, and no ears other than Brother McCauley were there to hear. For this room…this room was a godless place.

Within the circle of candles, Brother McCauley sat. He sat and turned his mind inward and upward, and he prayed. He prayed with more conviction than he ever had in his life. For upon his prayers, he carried the souls of the dead.

He prayed for their salvation. He prayed for their release. He prayed for God to heal this broken land and to accept their souls into the kingdom of heaven.

And then, all at once, there was a blast of cold air, and the candles flickered out. No longer could Brother McCauley see, or hear, the dead. He was simply alone in the dark prayer room. And there he sat in the silence of a job done well for several minutes.

At last, he stood, gathered his supplies, and walked toward the door to the prayer room. He pushed against the door, but the door would not budge. He pushed harder, still, nothing. He threw his entire shoulder into the door, but still the door would not move. He pounded his fists but heard no sound until, in his despair, he began scratching, clawing at the door for release.

All that he could hear was a faint scratch, scratch, scratch.

The official report of the Brothers of the Monastery of Good Hope is that Brother McCauley died of natural causes, as there were no signs to contrary. His heart simply stopped, as hearts sometimes do. No one was sure why he was in the prayer room when it happened, surrounded by candles, which had all melted by the morning when he was found. No one is sure why his fingernails were curled back and broken. All that they know is that he was buried outside the monastery in the small graveyard, under a stone bearing only his name and Psalm 23:6.

"And I will dwell in the house of the LORD forever."

Vague

I can't write poetry vague enough
that my love poems could be about anyone,
so I guess that I don't have a career as a
Valentine's Day card writer.
I try to be vague,
to give some generic description
about the softness of your skin,
but I can't stop there because all I remember
is the way your body felt after you put on your coconut
body lotion,
the way the smell would linger on my fingers
when I would run them down your spine.
I try to write about your blue eyes
(which already alienates part of the audience),
but I always make it worse
by talking about the way they'd light up
when we would have photoshoots wearing silly hats
or how you would throw your arms in the air
at the beach.
I could write about your voice,
but then I would have to mention
the thrill in my heart whenever I would
hear you sing
at the old dingy bar
that is the last place I ever had a drink.
Or perhaps sleeping next to you at night,
but then I would be mentioning when you woke up in
the middle of the night
and needed me to help calm you down
or check to make sure
there were no murderers in the apartment

(there never were).
I could write of
travels,
sunflowers,
airports,
green hills,
or city streets.
But as you can see,
my poetry can't fit just anyone,
because my only audience is you.

Pea Crisps

I still don't know
if it's the taste I like
or if it's the memory
of lying next to you in the grass
tasting the salt lingering on your lips.

An Essay about Love

Today, I want to talk about something that may seem a bit funny for me to be talking about right now: *Love.*

The thing that many of us forget, and that makes all the difference in the world, is that love is a choice. There is nothing binding you to that feeling. No one can force you to love them. And as such, love isn't anyone's fault but yours.

Many of us, and I have been guilty of this in my past as well, feel that you "need" that person in your life, their love in your life. That without it, you are nothing. But the truth is much more beautiful than that. We don't *need* anyone. We can survive without that person in our life. But what we've chosen is that we want to spend our life and time with that person. We've chosen that we want to feel those feelings and specifically that we wanted to share those feelings with this other person. And that choice, that decision, is far better of a connection than any "need." Your partner isn't food or water or shelter. Your partner is someone you have chosen to include in your life.

And we need to remember this for several reasons. The main reason is that this means that we've chosen to accept them as they are. This doesn't mean unconditional love, where it doesn't matter what they do, we'll always just let them get away with it. What it means is that we've chosen that the work required in learning to make them feel appreciated and loved is worth it. It means that we're willing to learn their love language and how to show them how you care…not on your terms, but on theirs. It shows that you're willing to make (minor) changes in your lifestyle to accommodate them. It means that you're choosing to make room in your life for that person. Note that this doesn't mean giving up all of yourself for them.

The other reason this is important to remember is so we pull our heads out of our own asses sometimes. If we made the choice to love this person, why are we not making as much room for them in our lives as we can? Why aren't we doing the work to make them feel appreciated and loved? If you don't know the answer to those questions, it might be worth dwelling on…because your partner definitely will. Because if you aren't making room in your life for your partner or working on things that are trouble spots in your relationship, then of course your partner is going to assume that this means that you are *choosing* not to love them as much, or at all. Wouldn't you feel that way if your partner didn't make room in your relationship for you?

So today, recognize that you're choosing to love. Recognize *who* you're choosing to love. And show it to them. Maybe it's figuring out their love language (if you're not familiar with them, there's a lot of good information online about them…hint, there are five of them!). Maybe it's making a change in your life that your partner has been asking you to make. Maybe it's making more room in your life for them. Maybe it's as simple as telling them that you love them and holding them. Listen to your partner's expression of their love and listen to how the choices you're making every day express your love to them.

Don't let yourself get in the way of making sure that your partner knows that you're choosing them. And never forget that your love is your choice.

Good Things—Essay

I have finally reached the point that I view what happened a few months ago as a good, necessary thing. That I recognize that I needed something to wake me up and look at myself honestly and start making changes. Not that I'm happy that it happened. Not that I have found a way to forgive myself for not changing sooner. Not that I'm glad certain people have left my life or that I don't wish more than anything that they would decide to come back into it. But that I recognize that it needed to happen.

I was sliding deeper and deeper into my depression, alcoholism, and my distracting coping mechanisms. I wasn't doing anything to better myself. And I know that if it had kept sliding the way it was, I probably wouldn't have been able to stop it. Another year of treating myself as I had been, and I probably wouldn't have been able to pull myself out when I started spiraling, and I probably wouldn't have survived it. So it saved my life. As much as it hurt, as much as it still hurts…at least I'm still alive, and more than that… I've found a way to thrive.

I do so many things that I never thought I would be able to do. I've started meditating regularly. I've started doing yoga (I have my second class today, at my gym to see if I need a membership to a yoga studio specifically or if my gym yoga is good for what I need as well). I listen to myself and my needs, and I respect them. I've been working out consistently and eating better and am in the best physical shape of my life. I've been writing consistently again. I've started writing music, which isn't to a point where I'm ready to share it, but it's getting there! I've had some incredibly difficult conversations with people that in the past I probably would have hid from or reacted poorly to the situation. I understand myself better than I ever have in my life.

And I know I'm not going to stop. It's not just the momentum I've built up of change in my life—it's how I feel. I feel *good*. I feel better than I ever have in my life because I'm dealing with things and not just running from them. That doesn't mean I'm happy all the time, per se. It means I'm okay with not always being happy. That I can take those "negative" emotions like anger, sadness, regret…and use it as a catalyst for change. I can learn from what they're telling me and do the work that I need to make it easier for me. I can grow, and I can be better than I've been in the past.

And the learning I've done hasn't only been internal. I've been finding better ways to communicate with family and friends. Learning how to talk about what I'm feeling and going through. Learning to listen beyond just the words but into the meaning behind them. I've been more present. And I can carry that into every relationship I have—familial, platonic, or romantic. And I've been approaching romantic relationships (mentally) better as well. In the past, I have always had issues seeing past a failed relationship, thinking I would never be able to find another in the future. Or, conversely, jumping into a new one way too soon and hurting everyone involved. But I no longer feel that way. I know that I'm at least not a horrible person and will be able to be in a relationship again. But I also understand that's not where I am right now and am learning to love myself until I'm ready. I don't know when that will be, and I don't know who it will be with, but I know no matter what that I will be my best self and will be able to be a better partner than I have been in the past.

It feels good to know myself. It feels good to be growing. To be better. I don't know what the future is going to be, and that's okay. That's healthy. I've learned to give up the control I needed to feel. I've learned to give up drinking. I've learned to enjoy the present. I've learned. And that's not something I could do before.

Yellow, Red, Gray, and Green

I remember the first time
that I saw someone get shot,
bright yellow flash
followed by red,
so much red,
covering the large screen
of the movie theater wall.
It was...
nothing.
Maybe a little startling
for a child,
but no one else in the theater
seemed to mind.
My father didn't react;
hell,
he even seemed to cheer,
in his own way.

Well, I've seen many people die
at this point in my life.
Gunshot gray skin,
knife red arterial spray,
serial killer green.
The bodies pile up
and block out the light of the silver screen.

But that still never prepares you
for watching a body stand on the edge
of the parking garage
across from work,
standing and talking

and you hope,
yes, you hope,
that maybe words
can finally fill
their hopeless void
with enough blue sky
to lift their leg over the rail.
The silver screen
doesn't prepare you for when they
let go in real life.
It doesn't prepare you
for the fact that when a body
drops from the sixth floor of
a parking garage,
and gains velocity on the eighteen-degree drop,
that the body will bounce
upon impact.
It won't prepare you for the
cracked skull red ooze
on the gray pavement.
The silver screen
never shows you the splatter
being cleaned from the sidewalk
with a firehose
and running down the
streets
into the sewer—
bits of teeth
and brains
and blood
and life
slowly swirling down the city's drains.

But the red.
The red.
The red they got right.

Taking Pictures

I wish that I could show you
what I see,
the hidden glow in your eyes
and the love in your smile.
I wish I could make your heart beat
the same way mine does
when your fingers brush my skin,
or when I feel my phone buzz
a message from you.
I wish that I could take your breath
the way that you do when you walk in
wearing your long red dress
and your smoldering eyes,
or when you spin around in joy
enjoying the ocean air around you.
I wish that you could see yourself
the way that I see you.
Feel you.
Breathe you.
So I'll keep taking pictures of you,
so that maybe one day you'll see
what I see.

Meditations of You

Breathe in.
Breathe out.
Breathe in deeper this time.
Where do you feel the breath move?
Is it in your stomach, or is it in your chest?
Or maybe even in the small of your back,
especially if you're curled on your side.
Now think, but don't, about clearing your mind
and find that silence.
That silence inside of you.
I find mine, I feel mine,
I breathe mine…
But I find no silence.
I find only you,
and I breathe in only you,
and I feel my breath in my heart.

The Mother and Her Dead Daughter
Or
Amelia and Her Mother

Mary Jane Devae lost her daughter when she was only six weeks old. The daughter I mean, not Mary Jane. She came down with a case of the black fever, which she never passed to her mother, though she was still suckling at the time. She was buried in a plain wooden box under the oak tree behind the old family home, with very little to do, as Mary Jane and her husband were not very affluent, and anyway, it does not make financial sense to waste money on a child who had hardly lived long enough to have a name.

But she did have a name. It was Amelia.

Three months passed, twice the time that Amelia had drawn breath. In that time, Mary Jane and her husband grieved, as one does, and carried on with their lives, as just as death does not stop for you, neither does the world stop for death. And so, after the first week, her husband began leaving for the market each morning, leaving Mary Jane alone to stare out the window at the oak tree, as the small mound of dirt slowly sprouted grass and was lost to the green sea of the yard. All that remained visible was the small wooden cross that they had built to mark the site.

One night, some months later, as Mary Jane slept in the darkness, she had a dream, but the dream was as vivid as anything she had ever seen in her waking mind. She was lying in her bed, as she did every night, but felt small hands and feet crawling along her legs under the covers. Small, cold hands. And when they reached her breast, she felt a toothless, sunken mouth begin to drink from her, in the place where such things are done. And in the dream, the mouth drank insatiably, and Mary Jane could feel herself emptying, slowly draining away the very essence of her soul, or so the priest would have said. And after a time, she was left as nothing.

She awoke with a start and went to the mirror in the washroom, for she felt a small pain upon her chest. When she looked upon the bare skin, she found a small bruised ring around her nipple as if a small, toothless mouth had attached itself to her.

A cold shiver ran down the back of her neck, but still she returned to her bed. For the rest of the night, she was unable to sleep though nothing else disturbed the silence of the empty home, save her husband's snoring.

In the morning, she did not repeat the story of her dream to her husband for fear that he would think her mad with grief. Instead, she held her tongue, and once he had washed and left for the market, she stole away to the oak tree in the yard, where she had not dare tread for the past three months.

At the foot of the tree, she inspected the earth but found it undisturbed, with new sprouts of grass covering the small mound. The small wooden cross still stood in the earth, as it had when her husband had struck it into the earth three months past. She returned to the home and began the daily wash but found her mind occupied with thoughts of the night before.

For the next few days, there were no more dreams, good nor bad, to disturb Mary Jane's slumber. And as time passed, her memory of the dream began to fade with the bruise upon her chest. She had pushed the dread memory from her mind, when, on the fifth day after, she found herself in a dream again.

Or was it a dream? Either way, she found herself awake on the bed in the dark. Beside her, she could hear her husband slumbering away. And at her feet, she could feel tiny, cold hands reaching forward, grasping at her toes.

Frozen in terror, she felt as those hands slowly, blindly, lurched forward, felt the weight of cold legs pushing forward, hungrily reaching further up her body. With each frozen breath, she felt the weight upon her inch closer and closer and closer, until eventually, she felt that toothless mouth latch upon her in the same spot as before, felt the same draining of her life force slipping through her breast. Mary

Jane wanted to reach forward, to reach out, to stop the mouth from draining her to nothing. But she lay still, too overwhelmed with fear to move. And so, for a second time, she felt her life force drain from her body.

In the light of the next morning, she found that the bruise, which had almost faded away was fresh and raw once more. She could almost see the gum line of the toothless mouth on her skin. And so she resolved to tell her husband and thus spoke to him while she served him his breakfast before leaving for the market.

"I have a fresh bruise upon my breast, where I have been suckling a babe in my dreams," she told him. "I believe it to be our child, our Amelia."

Her husband looked up, a combination of grief and pity crossing his eyes. "Our Amelia has been dead for some thirteen weeks now. Dead and buried and in the great after beyond our reach, and beyond the reach of you. I know that her loss has taken its toll, and I know what great grief you must feel, for I feel it too, but our daughter has not been visiting you in the night. You must let her go."

"I know what I've felt, and I have found a fresh bruise after each visit. It is not just a dream, or my body would not show the marks of this visitation."

"You are losing what sense you had to this grief, and I have tolerated it long enough. Here, if our child has been returning in the night, let us both venture to the grave where we lay her to rest, and so lay this matter to rest once and for all." And finishing his last bite, he stood and walked into the yard behind, Mary Jane walking shortly behind.

The pair strode across the small yard and to the oak tree, with the small mound in front of it. The grass still lay unperturbed, but the wooden crucifix which had been struck deeply into the ground just days before lay flat upon the earth, and no longer stood tall over the marked grave. The two looked around the tree for any signs of disruption but found no other.

"The cross, see, it lays flat when last night, it stood where you struck it into the ground!" Mary Jane picked up the cross and held it toward her husband.

"There is no mystery here. Some animal crossing through the yard must have brushed aside it and toppled it to the ground. Or the wind blew while we slept and knocked it flat." And so said, he went and retrieved his mallet and struck the cross into the ground again, deeper this time.

And without another word, he gathered his lunch and left for the market for the day, leaving poor Mary Jane alone with her delusions.

That day, Mary Jane sat in her armchair, gazing out the window at the tree, leaving but for scant moments to relieve herself and eat. But though she sat all day long, nothing passed through the yard, nor did anything stir beneath the tree, and it was such that her husband found her when he returned that evening.

The next few days were strained in the household, with Mary Jane scarcely speaking and her husband simmering with misplaced anger at her grief. But for all the strangeness in the home, Mary Jane was not visited in the night for two weeks, though this reprieve did nothing to still the unrest in her mind. Every night before she slept, she lit a candle and left it burning by her bed, to see anything or any-one that might enter the room.

Her sleep was fitful, and she awoke each morning feeling unrested, each day more so than the last. She haunted her home, staring out the window whenever she passed, staring at the old oak tree and the ground beneath. In fact, as the week turned to two, her skin had paled and slackened, as her eyes grew deep and sunken, and she found her head bobbing with slumber as she performed her duties around the home.

And so, she found herself, some thirteen days after the last inci-dent, with fever and an overwhelming exhaustion that fed through her body. The doctor was called, and after letting some blood, as was the custom, told her to lay in bed and rest, lest the fever take stronger hold. And so she was put in bed, while her husband left for market for the day.

At first, she was too afraid to sleep, haunted by memories, and mindlessly toying at the spot on her chest where the bruise had been.

But as the day wore on, she found her eyelids drooping, eventually closing, and fell into a deep slumber.

She was awoken by the feeling of something on her chest. Something without any teeth, suckling upon her breast. And as light crept through the cracks in the sash, she could see a mound under the blanket. Caught with fear, but empowered by the light of day, she raised her sickly hand and threw the bed dressing wide.

In that instant, she saw her child, dear Amelia, dirt beneath her fingernails, and gray, cracked, rotted skin, suckling upon her breast, as she had while she still lived. Amelia's skin was a sunken gray, and when she looked up at her mother, Mary Jane realized that her eyes had fallen into the back of her skull, and there was the faint smell of rotting flesh billowing out.

Mary Jane promptly passed out.

When she awoke, the sun was beginning to dim behind the horizon, and she found herself alone in a silent home. A fresh bruise, with just a faint drop of blood, was visible upon her skin. She quickly rose from her bed and strode to the yard, where she found the cross once more lying upon the ground and the grass in perfect placement. She walked hesitantly, scared of what she might find, but as she approached, she found nothing more out of the ordinary.

Or was there? The tree bark just above the mound had scrapes, deep scrapes, as if tiny fingernails had dug into them, using it to pull itself from the earth.

She recoiled, fear shooting through her arm, bile rising in her throat. She ran and retrieved a trowel, fell to her knees, and began digging, digging, throwing dirt behind her, over her, clawing madly at the dirt to dig deeper and deeper.

Her husband returned home an hour or so later and found the home still quiet. He didn't think to look out the window at the tree but instead walked to the bedroom to check on his wife.

When he entered the room, he found her rocking in a chair, with her back to him, singing a soft song beneath her breath. As he began to speak, she shot a "shh…" his way and slowly turned toward him.

As she turned, he saw that she clutched the gray and half-rotted corpse of their daughter, held close to her breast, as if feeding her as she had when Amelia were alive. Mary Jane's eyes stared as if any life force she once had was lost completely from her body. But still she rocked softly back and forth, singing sweet lullabies under her breath.

At Midnight

I've traded in the parties
for sipping cocoa in the cold
and watching the festivities from afar
as the clock ticks another second,
like any other second,
but carries with it a whole new year.
I've traded my champagne,
since I stopped drinking in the old year,
for cuddles with my cat
and waiting by the phone
hoping to get even just one text
from you to know
you might still care.
I've traded in almost
every part of the old me,
piece by piece,
built up over the old year.
But even then,
you're still the only person that I want to kiss
at midnight.

New Year—Essay

Well, 2019 is officially coming to a close. And while I don't really care all that much about the new year, I still find myself being reflective. A lot has happened in the last year. A *lot*. And, frankly, I didn't expect to see the end of 2019. Even once things started going better for me, I was still worried that I was going to slide back into old habits and into that bad mental state. But I haven't, and at this point I honestly don't think I will again.

I still get *sad*, obviously. We all do that. And I have quite a few things going on in my life in the last six months that I think it's understandable that I'm sad sometimes. But I'm not *depressed*. I don't fall into a pit of despair. I don't feel like my life is insurmountable. Are there things that I want to be different? Yes. Are there people that I want in my life to meet the new version of me? Of course. But I've gotten better about accepting life as it is and moving through everything.

When I look back at the person I was a year ago, I hardly recognize myself. I was so lost, angry, hurting, and was just flailing to try to find any comfort that I could. But the flailing was just more hurt, more hurt that I was sending to others. But now I'm a completely different person. Not even just a little different, different to the point that I hardly recognize myself. And that feels amazing.

And when I say I'm a different person, I don't just mean that I stopped drinking, started meditating, doing yoga, or going to the gym. I mean that I have changed my entire outlook on life. I don't only see the terrible things in my life and in the world. I don't fight against those feelings inside of me… I allow myself to process them and feel the sadness, happiness…whatever. I found a way to live in the moment, and in doing so, I opened up this huge pocket of love and care that I had hidden and squished deep down inside of myself.

I'm not perfect. And I know that there's no way to rewrite my history and make myself this person in the past. But what I can do, what I *have* done, is to grow into a person that will never make those same mistakes again. I took what I felt and learned from it. I took the time to put myself in other people's shoes and to learn the skills that I lacked. I learned to listen more actively. I learned to experience the people around me. I learned how to better approach relationships or habits that I had that were impacting how I interacted with others. And I changed them. Or, at least, I am actively changing them (life is kind of a keep learning and growing kind of thing). And I am so happy that I have.

So here's to 2020—a year of active listening. A year of working for the crisis text line and supporting those in need of help. A year of working on my writing and continuing to grow at work. A year of continued growth, without hiding from my feelings with distractions and alcohol. A year without any more suicide attempts. A year of being me.

Resolutions—Essay

A new year is starting up! And while I'm not a big fan of "new year resolutions," I thought that I would offer some advice that worked for me in case anyone is looking for any! My life has changed so, so much in the last six months, and I have made so many changes that have benefitted my mental health, and I know that you can as well if it's what you're looking for!

- Meditate or do yoga—Seriously, I cannot stress enough how life changing this has been for me. Even a few minutes a day can help you understand your mind better and center you.
- Clean—This one is hard. I'm not 100 percent sure if I'm cleaning because I'm in a better mental state or in a better mental state because I'm keeping my living space clean. Either way, it's definitely helpful for you. So fold the laundry when it comes out or take ten minutes to wipe down your kitchen counters. I know sometimes it's hard to convince yourself, especially in a depressive episode, but the movement can help get you rolling.
- Exercise—Even if it's walking. Just move. Get your blood flowing. It really does help. And it doesn't need to be a *lot* of movement, like going to the gym. Just do something.
- Cut back on caffeine (and alcohol)—This is all about moderation. I'm not saying they're bad for *you* but think about the amount of them that you drink. Do you feel anxious or depressed when you drink them a lot? Just listen to your body about what you need here.
- Read—Really, read whatever you want. Reading helps activate your mind and your imagination. But there are also some *amazing* self-help books out there, about everything from relationships to communication to how we talk to

ourselves. Use the help from experts on what you're trying to accomplish instead of trying to reinvent the wheel.

- Take time for yourself—This is something I still struggle with from time to time. Don't stay so busy that you don't have time to relax and do things you love. Whether it's a quiet hour reading on the couch or a bath, take time to slow down.

- Journal—Future journaling is an amazing way to realize your goals. It's basically a way for you to write where you want to be so that your mind wires itself to think that's how things really are. I do this every night before bed.

- Grateful journaling—I do this daily as well. Just write down three things you're grateful for. This will allow you to see the good in your life. There are always things to be grateful for—from friends and family down to a good cup of tea on your balcony. Remind yourself of the good things in your day so that you don't only dwell on the bad.

- Candles—Get some. They're awesome. And add a nice amount of energy into your living space (not, like, hippy energy, though also that, but, like, literally, fire is motion and energy).

- Find a hobby—What do you love doing? Drawing? Knitting? Playing the kazoo? Whatever it is, even if it's something you don't think you're good at...do it. You'll get better as you go, and you'll be filling your time with something that you find fulfilling.

- Make a check list—I print a monthly check list and post it on my wall. Do I get everything done on it? No. But it reminds me what I want to accomplish each month so I can work toward it.

- Figure out what you Give a Fuck About—Make a list of the ten to twenty things you care about. Like, really care about. Where do you want to be putting your energy? Find whatever that is for you. This will make it easier for you to say "no" to other things because you know they're not on your list. Post this somewhere you can see every day to remind yourself.

- Remember yourself—Remember that you don't *need* to change. You're an awesome person. If you have things that you want to change, focus on them. But do it for you. Don't do it because someone else wants you to or because you think it will make someone think differently of you. Don't waste your time of changes for other people; that won't leave you with the energy for things that matter to *you*.

How Many Times

How many times,
how many times,
how many times did I have
the chance to change,
and just stayed the same,
repeating and repeating and repeating,
a locked groove repeating my worst
actions again and again and again
and never changing,
never doing what I needed.
How many times
did you ask me,
plead with me,
to save myself.
But I just sat there
sinking and sinking
deeper under water
until I couldn't breathe
and I almost pulled you under.

I Remember You

I remember you
in the office,
your feet curled up under your legs
as you wrote and edited and laughed.
I remember your laugh the most.
Telling me you'd steal my shoes,
or of Brian Fallon's songwriting,
and all of the things going wrong
in your life.

I remember you
and your best friend
on your Facebook messenger
sending me stupid nothings
and pretending that you didn't have
a schoolgirl crush on me,
but not pretending very well.

I remember you
leaving,
remember the longing as I watched you walk away
but knowing it was what you needed.
And I remember telling you
to keep in touch,
dear god how I wanted you to keep in touch.

I remember you
at night when the monsters of your mind and shadows
were strongest
talking to me about every secret
that I would never repeat where anyone

could read them.
I remember those talks
the most.
Remember how strong you were
for slaying your beasts
day after day.

I remember you
telling me about the boy you liked,
the boy you dated,
the boy that wasn't me.
I remember every word
over those long years
when you were just
a name and a picture on a screen.

I remember you.
And I remember that I loved you,
even then,
even when I couldn't find the words
and I didn't even realize myself
and you never knew…
I remember loving you.

It's a Lego, Lego, Lego, Lego World

*T*he scene opens on a living room, neatly deco-
rated with a homey feel. It is nighttime. There is
a small town of Lego houses, people, and cars in
the center of the room—seemingly left there from a
child earlier. We hear a door open.

*Enter RICHARD. RICHARD is obviously heavily
intoxicated. He is wearing his clothes from the bar
and has a stain from a spilled drink down the front
of his shirt. He wanders into the room and drops his
keys on a table, missing the table and dropping them
on the floor. He drunkenly bends down to pick up
the keys and places them on the table.*

*RICHARD walks further into the room and steps
onto the Lego town. The pieces scatter everywhere
as he trips, causing more damage to the town. The
pieces crash loudly.*

RICHARD
Fuck! Fucking piece of shit toys.

*RICHARD, in his drunken anger, kicks the Legos
and scatters them further.*

*Enter EUGENE. EUGENE is RICHARD's adult
son, who has autistic disorder. This is a serious dis-
order and should in no way be played for laughs.
Because don't be a dick.*

EUGENE

Dad? My world! You destroyed my world!

RICHARD

It was sitting in the middle of the floor. How many fu… How many times have I told you not to leave your toys lying in the middle of the floor?

> *EUGENE doesn't respond and kneels down on the ground and starts working on picking up the pieces and meticulously putting them back. RICHARD, his anger slowly dissipating, sits down and starts taking his shoes off.*

EUGENE

I left them out so that we could play when you got home. But you didn't come home before Mom put me to bed.

RICHARD

I… I'm sorry. I ended up getting caught up with the guys and didn't realize the time.

EUGENE

Mom said you were just getting drunk because you're too stubborn to deal with your own problems.

RICHARD

Well, your mom's one to talk. Maybe if she spent a little more time caring about…

> *Beat.*

I won't do it again.

EUGENE

You've said that before.

RICHARD

I'm sorry I destroyed…stepped on your little world.

EUGENE

It's okay. They're Legos. You can put them back together.

RICHARD

Here, let me help.

RICHARD crouches down and starts helping.

EUGENE

No, that piece doesn't go there! That's the fire station, not the school!

RICHARD

Oh, I'm sorry! I didn't know. Where does…this piece go?

EUGENE

Over here. That's Dr. Jakob's house. That's why it's blue.

RICHARD

It's really nice of you to include your therapist's house in your town.

EUGENE

Everyone's here! This is our house. And over here I put your work. And that's Mommy's work. And that's the bar that you always go to. And this one is you.

EUGENE holds up a Lego figure that is holding a beer mug.

I even gave him a beer glass!

RICHARD

That's…very thoughtful, Eugene.

EUGENE

I like building Legos with you, Daddy. I wish we did it more often.

RICHARD

I'm sorry, Eugene. I wish we could, too. I just have so much going on. You know... Daddy stuff. Work and grocery shopping and chores.

EUGENE

But why do you have to be gone for so long? You left this morning and didn't come back until tonight. Don't you like playing Legos with me?

RICHARD

You know I like playing Legos with you. You know I love you, Eugene. It's just...it's a lot sometimes.

EUGENE

I'm sorry that I'm a lot.

RICHARD

That's not... No, Eugene, this isn't...this isn't your fault.

EUGENE

Okay, Daddy.

RICHARD

It's... It's not anyone's fault.

EUGENE

If you say so.

The two continue putting pieces back together for a moment in silence. Eventually, RICHARD is struggling to put a piece on a building and starts pushing too hard, and the building collapses again.

RICHARD

Fucking thing! Why do they make it so goddamn hard. This is for children for Christ's sake!

EUGENE

Picks up the piece that RICHARD was trying to put on and puts it onto another building. EUGENE notices the underhanded jab that RICHARD had in the last line but chooses to ignore it.

Here. This can be the fire station now.

RICHARD

I thought you said that was the school.

EUGENE

It was, but sometimes when Legos fall apart, you can't get them back together the same way. It's just how Legos are. That's why I like them. It doesn't matter if I break them, because I just build something new.

RICHARD

I wish that life was more like Legos sometimes.

EUGENE

Why don't you just make it more like them?

RICHARD

That's not really how it works, Eugene.

EUGENE

Why not? Maybe it's just that nobody has tried it yet.

Beat.

I'm tired, now. Thanks for playing with me, Dad. I'm going to go back to bed. We can finish tomorrow when you're feeling better.

Mom said you should sleep on the couch tonight and think about what you care about. Sweet dreams.

> *EUGENE stands and then bends to kiss RICHARD on the forehead.*
>
> *RICHARD looks very much like the child here. EUGENE exits.*
>
> *RICHARD drunkenly stands up. He softly nudges the Legos out from beneath his feet and then collapses to sit on the couch. He looks at the Lego town for a moment, then sighs and falls backward into a lying position.*

Lights down.

Lettuce

I can't see lettuce
the same anymore,
ever since you put it on your head
and danced around the kitchen.
I can't see lettuce as anything
other than the love
of an absurd woman
filled with all the laughter
of the world.

World Suicide Prevention Day—Essay

Today is World Suicide Prevention Day. Clearly, this year this day means something a little different to me. I also, fittingly, set up an appointment to get my semicolon tattoo today, not realizing that today was Suicide Prevention Day. Happy accident, that.

I want to take today to talk about suicide in a slightly different light than it's normally portrayed. Instead of from the outside of it and talking about all the things you can do to help someone, I want to give the inside perspective, what was going through my mind when I made the decision to kill myself.

I think many of us have had people close to us who have committed suicide or attempted or struggled with suicidal ideology. And from the outside, it seems like maybe a selfish decision. Or maybe you wonder what signs you could have seen or wonder what you could have done to prevent it. Or maybe you think, "That person didn't really have a reason to do that or feel that way" (if you're that type of person, you're an asshole, and maybe you should read some books on psychology or empathy, but I digress). From the outside, it's easy to attribute blame, or if not easy to do, at least makes it easier to cope with.

But suicide, and depression and anxiety in general, are horrible darkness that sit inside you. It doesn't matter what's happening in that moment. The thoughts of failure, helplessness, anger—whatever the specific feeling is—seem so overwhelming that there doesn't seem to be another way out. It seems that your options are either to suffer forever or suffer greatly for a short time but then be free of that suffering. It's not selfish—it's easy. And it's never a decision that's made lightly. It's a decision made after struggling for a long time, when you've tried everything you can think of, everything you can do, but still feel that way. You're exhausted and all you want is for the pain to stop. And then there's this solution to that, a way to make sure that the pain won't be able to continue for another day. And so you take it.

Everyone's experience is different. Maybe you're doing it because you feel unloved. Maybe you have immense physical pain or sickness. Maybe you just literally can't fathom the future. But they all kind of boil down to the same issue of helplessness, of not being able to see a better life in the future. Whether this is based on facts or not isn't important; all that matters in that moment is that you think it.

So now to discuss what was going through my mind when I made the decision. I've struggled with depression and anxiety for as long as I can remember. Literally. My mom used to tell me I was going to die of a heart attack by the time I was ten years old, so that may give you an idea of how long this has been going on. Looking back, that should have been a big clue to myself that I had massive anxiety and depression issues that I was already internalizing, but I was ten and didn't know words like *internalizing* yet. As I got older, I hid from it as much as I could, chasing highs like video games, alcohol, pizza, ice cream…whatever would quiet my mind. But it wasn't really quieting; it was just sweeping everything under the rug. And my rug was getting so full that it looked like an ant hill was building up under it.

I've also never been good with loss. The problem with having a lot of friends and big families is that a lot of people die around you. I've had friends and family die from natural causes, suicide, drug overdoses, car accidents, murder…things caused by people and things completely out of anyone's control. I've seen people die way too young and people whose deaths were probably for the best. But none of them were easy. And this just added to my growing pile under my rug, year after year.

Not to mention the issues that I see in my friends and family right now. Watching people slowly succumb to illnesses, destroy their lives with continued decisions to live places that were causing them harm, and being completely helpless to do anything. And so I continued to feel that helplessness and felt that nothing would ever get better. That there was nothing that could ever happen to make the world a better place because no matter what I did, those things would never change. And I'd have to just keep watching them. And I couldn't do it anymore.

On top of that, I felt alone. Now, I know that people will always say "You're not alone" or "You can always reach out." If you've never suffered from depression, you don't understand that in those moments you don't think like that. And those statements actually start to feel extremely fake when people say them to you, because you feel lonely all the time, even when you're at a coffee shop with friends or with your partner. You just always feel like you're the only one in that situation, the only one who knows how you feel, the only one who actually cares about you. And that's the worst, because then you start vilifying the people around you, because you still feel lonely, so it must be something wrong with them not helping you. Because if it's something wrong with you, that's scarier. Because if it's something wrong with you, nothing you do will ever make that go away.

So I felt alone and tired and helpless and unhelpful. I felt lost and couldn't think of what my life would be the next week, let alone the next year or beyond. And it all just fell on me. I knew there were people who loved me and would miss me, but in that moment, it didn't matter. I knew that there would be some good moments again at some point, but the darkness was so overwhelming that those moments didn't seem worth wading through to get there. I knew that it was a permanent solution as well—that was the fucking point. I knew that even losing out on all the good things, at least I would finally stop having the bad.

That's really what it is. I think people look at suicide as a loss of hope. It's not. Suicide is when hope stops being enough. You can hope things will get better, but eventually "better in the future" isn't good enough. You need something to fix the problems now, and tomorrow, and any other bad thing that will happen. And that's how I felt. I knew there would be good things again, but I also knew there would be bad things. And at least if I was dead, I wouldn't have to worry about anything bad ever again.

I'm alive today. And I'm extremely happy to be here, making the improvements that I am, and rising out of my decision to take root as a whole new person, a better, more complete person. I'm finally facing my fears, my past, my thoughts, and myself. And I'm growing from it. But it hasn't been easy. And if I went back in time and told the me that made the decision to kill myself about what the future would hold for me two months in the future, I'd probably still make the same decision. Because it is hard to work your way out of that mental state. Extremely hard. And just "reaching out" or "thinking positive" isn't enough. It's a lot of self-reflection, habit changes, and learning. It takes a lot of alone time and a lot of time with people *actually* being there like they say they will be. It takes a lot.

If you're in that place now, I'm not going to tell you it gets better. Because it won't just get better. You have to make it better. But you *can* make it better. It takes work, and you have to do it every day, but you will make it better. You aren't alone, even though you feel like it. I promise others feel the exact same way. A lot more than you think.

And if you're someone who has a loved one who feels this way, reach out. They won't reach out to you, because they won't think they can. But don't just absently reach out. Reach out and actually listen to them and what they need. Maybe they just need you to listen. Maybe they just need you to be there. Maybe they need you to tell them a hard truth, and maybe they just need you to love them. That last one is almost always the case. But don't just reach out and leave it at that. Listen to what they say, and what they don't say. Actually be there, present in the moment with them.

So…happy World Suicide Prevention Day! I hope that everyone who is struggling keeps struggling. Because that's the only way we're going to get better.

The Plague by Albert Camus by Erik Keevan

The streets of Seattle
have been cut off from the world,
not by gates or walls
or even a police barricade
with spike strips.
No the streets
are quiet with fear,
choked back and jumping
at every cough
and dry throat.
The store shelves are empty,
not of orange juice and vitamins,
as they should,
but of hand sanitizer and toilet paper,
as if to suggest that no one washes their hands
or wipes their ass
when the world isn't ending.

The Plague by Albert Camus
says,
"There are more things to admire in men than to despise."
Yet the plague in that book
was spread by rats
of unknown origin,
where today everyone seems to know
that we should blame China for everything.
They take their fear
out on anyone their xenophobic
minds consider "Chinese,"

collapsing cheek bones,
bruising eyes,
and spitting vile refuse from their lips
(ironically,
spitting is far more likely to spread the virus
than a college student).
Camus got it wrong.
"Fear brings out the worst in humanity,
and it is fear that we should despise."

Light

You were the only light
in the darkness of my past life,
and I'm sorry that I dimmed your shine.
But I'm a roaring torch now,
darling,
and I want to set your soul on fire.

Surviving

We were both just trying to
survive
the best way we both
knew how.

But I don't want to survive
with you.
I want to live
with you,
with all of you,
and I want to see
life pouring
from your soul.

Candle

I have a candle.
It isn't anything much,
just a tall stalk of white wax
sitting in a tarnished lamp
with slight flecks of rust
around the edges.
My mother gave me the candle
when I was young—
placed it in the,
at the time,
shiny matte-black lantern
and lit the candle with a strike anywhere match.
I carried the lantern;
then,
alone,
my mother caught up with carrying her own
and trying desperately to keep her flame lit,
too distracted to keep mine—
and with the wind whipping through my home,
the candle flickered and
almost went out.

It was then,
many years later,
that I met someone who
used their own candle to help reignite
my own waning flame.
And, for a time,
my candle stayed lit,
my lantern bright and
illuminating my chest

and my mind
and my tongue.
But you cannot maintain
a flame by using another's,
or you will end with two burned-out wicks.
So she took her candle to another,
who was able to use their candle
to maintain hers.
And so it goes.

And so it went,
again and again,
where I would leave my lamp
open in the wind and
do nothing to protect the candle
and keep it lit,
bouncing from lit lamp
to lit lamp
just trying to keep myself aflame.

It came,
at last,
to a candle that made my own burn brighter
than ever before,
a candle that,
for once,
made me want to protect my candle
so that it could burn brightly
for years to come.
I came to finally view my candle
as a flame of love,
and not just a flame burning me
away from the inside.
But a desire to keep a wick lit
does not add length to a string,
nor does it stop the wax

from snuffing out the flame.
And so I stood, with my flame finally
lost,
with my lantern rusted closed,
and my mind cast so dark
that I forgot what the flame looked like.
And so I wrapped up the lamp,
the candle,
and all of my most important things
in an old towel, and threw it in the dumpster
behind my apartment.

And so it would have ended,
if not for my dumpster-diving friend
who pulled it out,
unwrapped it,
scrubbed the rust from the hinges,
and relit the candle inside,
using a little of their own candle.
And then another friend came
and added a little of their flame,
and another,
and another,
until I couldn't see the darkness anymore,
and my flame had grown brighter than it had ever before.
I am grateful for my flame,
now,
and I am grateful for
the people in my life
that lend me their flames
when mine starts to wane.
And I will use my flame
to light the candles
of those
who can't see anything except the darkness,
and one day,

all I will see
is a field of lanterns burning brightly
in the dark.

Cause, Choice, and Responsibility—Essay

I want to take a minute to talk about a few words that have been floating around my mind lately: *cause, choice*, and *responsibility*. This also ties directly into why I've been calling myself an asshole lately, which several people have tried to refute. I thank everyone who has in an attempt at supporting me. But you're wrong. And here's why.

Things happen in life. Some good, some bad, most of them kinda in the middle somewhere. And many of those things are completely beyond our control: death, natural disasters, winning the lottery. And one of the biggest things outside of our control is other people, and the choices they make. People decide to say things, to leave, to stay at your house when you just want to go to bed. You can influence these decisions, of course. You can be nice to people, and you can ask people to leave when you get tired. But you can't completely control them. These things that impact your life are *causes*. They cause you to feel, to react, to do something.

Did I have valid *causes* to feel the way that I did? Do I have valid reasons to think that people are going to just die suddenly, or leave me without saying anything, or not support me, or to think that the way that I am isn't the way that I'm supposed to be? You betcha. Those *causes* have been building up my entire life, from things other people have said, ways other people have treated me, cancer, car accidents, drug overdoses, and bad dates. All those things outside of my control have impacted my life and *caused* a reaction in me, caused me to be a certain way.

But the next part is the key part.

None of those things were *responsible* for how I felt. The responsibility of those emotions fell squarely on me, and from there, I made *choices*. I had my heart broken, so I *chose* to drink and eat pizza and wrap myself in a blanket and watch nothing but *Wilfred* for three weeks straight. People developed illnesses they would never recover from and would die far earlier than they deserved, and I *chose* to allow that to overwhelm me. And drink, of course, to feel better. And when people wanted me to stop, I *chose* to view that as an attack on me and respond defensively. Those were all my choices—no one else's.

I chose to do nothing proactive to help myself. My happiness was my own *responsibility* and not the responsibility of anyone else. Instead of doing things like I'm doing now—where I'm going to the gym, going on walks in new areas, meditating, exploring other types of therapy—I sat around and expected someone else to come in and make me happy. And drinking a lot to make myself "feel better." And then, when that didn't magically fix my problems, I placed the blame on others. It was the causes that had brought me to feel this way growing up or my job's fault or other people who didn't visit enough. But it wasn't my fault.

But thinking like that, and drinking like that, was my *choice*. I chose to drink constantly to feel better in the moment. I chose to sit around and play video games and do nothing else. I chose not to pursue my own mental health with the same veracity that I pursued alcohol. And my choice, in turn, hurt others because I wasn't doing what I needed to do. For myself and for those that I loved.

And that's why I call myself an asshole. Because I was the only one responsible for my actions, and I still made them. Because I have been an asshole.

I've fucked up. I've fucked a lot of things up, and I've hurt many people. Between my severe depression, my codependent habits, and my drinking, I'm sure that I've become a *cause* for many people, and I cannot ever express entirely how sorry that I am for that. I recognize what my actions and how my choices have impacted other people. I think I understand it more than people think that I do. When I say that I've been painfully honest with myself over the last few months, I mean that. The realizations that I have made and the things that I am holding myself accountable to have not been easy nor nice, but they have been necessary. To break my habit. To allow me to grow past the asshole I've been and grow into the…front hole that I'll be in the future.

I've been going through a lot of growth. And I've been a lot better about it. And I know that I will continue being even better than I am now. But it's only because I was honest with myself and took responsibility for my own actions. I am the person that has brought my life to the point where it is now. And as much as it sucks to say, it also gives me ownership so that I can change it. I'm not waiting for someone else to do it for me. I am the only one who gets to control me from now on.

Now, I definitely understand that depression, alcoholism, etc., are all real diseases. I understand that there are plenty of things outside of our control, even within our own minds and bodies. But when you start feeling crappy all the time, look at the choices that you're making and what you're doing to try and make yourself better. Be really honest with yourself. Because life sucks. But you don't have to.

Apologies—Essay

I wanted to talk about my post from the other day really quickly, where I once again apologized for my actions when I was lost in my depression and unhealthy coping mechanisms (i.e., drinking heavily, distracting myself to the point of oblivion, not expressing myself well, etc.).

One of the things that has always been an issue for me has been expressing myself in a valid way. I have felt unheard a lot in my life, for various reasons, and as my way of coping, I started to just not talk. If talking fell on deaf ears, what was the point? And then, of course, I started projecting that on everyone else, that talking about how I was feeling would just fall on deaf ears no matter who it was on the other end. So instead of reaching out for help, I dealt with things myself. Or more accurately, I didn't deal with things myself.

For me, life became about distraction. That was what life was about, just keeping myself distracted between the time that I woke up in the morning until I eventually died. So I fell into a pattern of distractible hedonism—drinking, playing video games, excessive masturbation…anything that would make it so that I wouldn't process the way that I was feeling, so that I could pretend that cloud of depression wasn't hanging over my head.

And that made it hard for me to have relationships. Not just romantic ones, but also friendships, family relationships, etc. When you try distracting yourself constantly, there's no space to live in the moment, to validly listen and pay attention to other people. And so I slowly destroyed those relationships by keeping myself distracted. Because the problem with not feeling heard and keeping yourself distracted is that it doesn't actually make you feel any better about it. It just makes you more miserable. And then you start acting out by saying things you don't mean or getting angry for seemingly no reason. Of course that hurts the other person, regardless of your intention.

It's that same depressive voice that I listened to every day, just going outward and hurting others.

I'm not saying this to make excuses for how I acted. Regardless of if you have a valid reason, it's never okay to hurt other people. That only perpetuates the problems and makes someone else feel them. It's our responsibility to help process our thoughts and emotions in a healthy way, so as not to impact others.

So I've been working hard to process things better. By meditation. By reading. By learning. By working in a focused manner with my therapist. By growing. Part of processing things, though, is feeling them. Not repressing those feelings, but diving headfirst into them, so that you can actually learn from them. Learn what you did wrong and how you can act differently in the future. I've been taking a meditation course on handling sadness on Head Space, and one of the things that the instructor said today struck me. Sometimes after working on it, you feel that sense of relief, that sense of happiness and spaciousness. And sometimes you feel the sadness. Because feeling the sadness is part of the process.

I have a lot of regrets. I have regrets of how I acted, how I hurt other people, how I caused people that I loved and still love dearly to leave. I don't blame them; I would have too. And yes, I'm angry at myself for getting to that point and not dealing with things earlier. I can't blame external things for how I acted, because even if I had valid reasons for feeling how I did, I could have and *should* have reacted differently. I can't change that now, but I can stop myself from doing it in the future. I can learn and be better every day. And I am.

But forgiving myself for doing that in the first place...that I don't think is a thing I can do. Because I should have known better. I should have created a healthy environment and given up my toxic traits. I should have listened more and grown earlier. I should have cared. So forgiving myself probably isn't going to happen. But I can use that feeling of regret to continue my journey. I can use the negative emotion to underscore what I don't want to do again. And yes, there are days when that regret will make me incredibly sad, where it will focus on the things I did and the things I lost. But it will also underscore the things that I won't do again, and eventually I can look back and see how far I've come, and then I can, maybe not forgive myself, but at least appreciate the changes that I've made in my life. Appreciate how much better I am. Appreciate that I've grown and am not that person anymore.

So thank you to the people who told me that I should forgive myself, and that those who love me have forgiven me. I appreciate the love and support comments like that show, even if I disagree that I should forgive myself. I'm holding myself accountable for my actions and for how I interact with the world, and I am no longer blaming others for how I act and feel. And that's my first step of healing.

There Is Wisdom

There is wisdom
in the drunk, depressed, alcoholic nihilist
sitting across from me at a coffee shop
on a Saturday night—
because we were supposed to hang out,
but I'm sober now
and so couldn't meet him at the bar that he has been at
since two in the afternoon.
He drinks a sobering coffee,
while I drink a calming rooibos
and pretend that I don't miss being able to meet him
at a bar and drink coffee
and stop all of the hard work that I'm doing to be better and
just settle back into my old routine
of drinking too much,
both alcohol and caffeine,
and sitting around in my underwear playing video games.

I don't miss it that often,
but on Saturday nights,
when the moon is full,
you can still hear the old alcoholic cry on the wind.

Talking is easy for him
and getting easier for me,
as it's what I've been working to do more of.
At first, it's music
and movies;
soon it has turned to
family illnesses,
broken hearts,

and my suicide attempt.
Why do we commit suicide?
Is it because we want to die?
A lot of people say that it is more that
we want to change.
But goddamn it,
my change was really a death.
I buried who I was
in the nation's smallest national park
which is also where I almost literally left my body
to return to the earth.

Am I better now?
What constitutes better?
I don't have deep dark depressive episodes anymore,
and I'm not as nervous constantly,
and I haven't cut myself in a while, which is good.
So I'd say I was better now than I was.
But I'm still alone,
and I can't undo my past,
no matter how far I travel from it,
and everyone tells me to just move on
and forgive myself.
But I haven't been able to find a way to do that yet.

My mind is wandering,
as it does.
Thinking.
I am working on my active listening ability,
so I return my attention to the moment,
and the moving lips of the drunk nihilist across from me.
He smiles.
He has a picture of a dick on his T-shirt
and tells me that I'm overthinking it.
That moving on isn't some big event;
it's the moments of happiness between the gaps of

loneliness,
that I shouldn't worry so much
because we're all just going to die at some point anyway,
and then it really won't matter.

I'm still not sure if that makes me feel better or not.

Who You Are Now

Who are you now?
Do you still have the same emerald soul,
and soft ocean eyes?
Do songs still spill from your lips
while your fingers tickle a song
across white and black steps?
Do you still wake
in the night
from your own vicious mind,
do you still watch TV with your legs
curled beneath you,
do you still worry about Jared Leto
stealing your clothes?
Who are you now?
For I know I am not the same person you knew,
and can only imagine neither are you.
If our souls crossed again,
would we even recognize ourselves?

Dear Past Erik

Dear past Erik,

I am sorry that that you were hurting for such a long time. I'm sorry that you felt unheard and useless and like you didn't matter. I'm sorry that you felt that you couldn't express how you were feeling and kept everything bottled up. I'm sorry that you felt unloved, and that you felt the need to drink to try and find some sort of peace. I'm sorry that no one saved you, and I'm sorry that it took me so long to realize that that's not how life works, and that we needed to save ourselves. I'm sorry that I didn't help you in a constructive way.

I know that you were doing what you thought you needed to do to survive. I know that you were only doing what you had learned as coping mechanisms and were trying to keep yourself alive. I know that you were only doing what you thought was best for yourself and were only trying to be happy. I know that you were lost, lonely, and scared. And I know that you never meant to hurt anyone.

I forgive you. I forgive you, and I promise you that I will not fall into those patterns again. I know now that there are so many better ways to express myself, and better reasons to want to live and experience the life around me. I know now that I don't need to keep myself constantly distracted to feel okay. I know now that I can love and be loved and appreciate and fully feel it. I know now that I don't need to be broken.

So thank you, past self, for surviving. Even if you didn't do it the best way. I know you didn't mean to hurt anyone—especially ourselves and those we cared about the most. Thank you, but I am also so glad that I'm not you anymore.

Dear past self, we got better.

Skin

It takes a beautiful soul
to smile
always,
even in the midst of the worst days.
For only one who has truly
been cut,
can understand the joy
of a scar long ago healed,
and can smile at the fresh skin
of a new tomorrow.

There's a Storm Coming In

She doesn't want to talk about it
but there's a storm coming in.
The salty air of the Sound
whips her hair,
and not for the first time,
I'm reminded that sirens
used to dash ships across the rocks—
not that this was the sirens' fault,
they were just who they were
and men who heard their songs
made their choices.

There's a storm coming in,
the water of the Sound,
normally so calm and placid,
has become frothy,
striking the rocky shore
and pulling away,
striking and away
a rhythm the ocean doesn't want
any more than the shore.
And yet still

there's a storm coming in.

She's on her phone,
and all I want is to send her an SOS
before my ship
dashes against her shore,
but I know,
I know,

it is too late—
the early storm bands are already here,
and the wind which whipped her hair
is caught in my sails.

There's a storm coming in,
and the frothy water
is now crashing against the shore,
shooting white foam across the path we used to walk,
as the water turns cloudy with the kicked-up sand
dragged from the ocean floor.
The silt and sediment and dead fish parts
sit stagnant on the stones
as she leaves the last time,
when I didn't even know that it would be the last time.
There's a storm coming in.

The water swells,
white capped and cold,
around my ankles as I walk home,
trying to ignore the storm crashing to my left,
neglecting the cold murky ocean
that has begun to engulf my feet—
pretending that my body isn't freezing.
But still I walk on,
because it's the only path that I have
to walk.

Home is no comfort,
for it's just as cold when I arrive,
and I find only an empty apartment
that should have been filled.
Well, not entirely empty, I suppose.

No,
there's a letter sitting on the coffee table,
just four simple sentences.
There's a letter sitting on the coffee table.

The storm is here.

The Land of No Land

One day,
she awoke to find
that her feet would no longer touch the ground.
No matter how she tried,
and make no mistake she did try,
they just wouldn't quite touch the earth.
And so she remained,
floating about an inch and a half above the carpet on her bedroom
floor.

Her mother came,
as did her brother,
and after them
the doctor,
a scientist,
a priest,
and an engineer.
But despite how they poked and prodded,
scanned and scoured,
none of those around her could discern what was stopping her
from staying firmly on the ground.

It was the engineer
who first proposed the idea
that perhaps they were looking at it backward,
that maybe there was nothing that
was making her float,
but rather that something had stopped holding her down.
And so it was that the floating woman
and the doctor,
and scientist,
and priest,

and engineer
changed their analysis—
that she was meant for somewhere other than here
and her soul had finally flown free.

And so it was that the engineer,
in her orange construction vest,
helped guide the floating woman
from her bedroom,
out of the house,
and onto the front yard.
Her mother packed a backpack—
with clothes, her daughter's favorite stuffed animal,
and a peanut butter and jelly sandwich
with the crust cut off.
Prepared for a journey,
the woman said thank you to the specialists who had helped,
bid her brother goodbye,
and gave her mother a tender kiss farewell.

And so,
her soul now completely unencumbered,
her feet began to lift higher—first a few inches,
then a few feet,
then dozens of yards,
and hundreds of yards,
thousands of feet,
until eventually she was floating
a mile from the surface of the earth.
And there,
her face shining with fragments of clouds,
she found others floating just beyond the horizon,
others whose souls had shaken off the weight of a weary soul
and had chosen to make their life in the sky.
And it is here that she found home—
in the land with no land.

Sober

I have been sober for almost
eight months.
Beyond that it will be nine,
ten,
a year,
two?
But there are no amount of drinks
that I can avoid
that will make up for the drinks
I drank
to cause the damage
that caused me to
stop drinking
in the first place.

They say to take it one day at a time,
and I do.
Honestly,
not drinking has been the easiest part of the last five months.
It's everything else that I now have to deal with.
Years of plaque buildup on
my mind,
scraping away little by little
armed with nothing but breathing,
a full night's sleep,
and silence.
I haven't had a craving for a drink that entire time,
I just keep working,
focused,
shining by mind into something new.

You told me that you had thought it was my drinking
but realized it wasn't.
But it was.
It was years of distraction
and escape
and self-abuse
and trying to numb my feelings until
I couldn't anymore and they boiled over.
It was years of never dealing,
never fixing,
never admitting.
But I have
and I will continue to scrub
my mind by processing these
hurts until I am whole
and clean again.
So I will take it one day at a time.
And then one week at a time,
a month,
a year.
But I can't help but think
how much easier this would be
if you were still here.

Sobriety—Essay

As I get closer to the one-year mark for my sobriety, I've been thinking a lot about the person that I was. The choices that I made. How I was feeling.

I didn't like leaning on alcohol. I liked being drunk (clearly, I wouldn't have done it if I hated it), but I did hate the fact that I kept falling into the same patterns over and over when I wanted to change. I think that's what most people don't recognize about people with addictions, very few of them *want* to have them. But it takes a lot of emotional support to get rid of something like that. A lot of hard work and understanding. Because to get past it, you have to get to the root of why you needed it in the first place.

For me, it was my depression. The emotional isolation that made me feel unloved and unsupported by everyone around me. That made me feel unheard. And I'm not going to lie, I still feel like I was. Part of that was that I was unable to communicate clearly and effectively about how I was feeling, but the conversations about my drinking were never about asking me how I felt, about what I needed… They were always angry condemnations of my actions and how they impacted others. Never about supporting me to get better.

Not that I'm saying I was right. This isn't me giving excuses for my actions. Honestly, I don't have any. Regardless of how I felt, I should have reacted better, reached out sooner, made the life changes that I've made now. I should have treated myself and the people I loved with more respect. But when I was there, when I was in it, I couldn't see that. I couldn't see what I was doing for what it was. I was just trying to dull the pain inside of me.

I'm not looking for forgiveness for the person that I was. Hell, I don't even forgive myself. I hate the person that I was, the things I did to try and make myself feel safe. I know I didn't mean it, but that doesn't fix the hurt I caused. All that I ask is for compassion for the person that I was and to recognize that the person I am now isn't him anymore. I'm not perfect. I know I still have things to work on. That's a lifelong process. But I am working on that, and I'm a hell of a lot better than I used to be.

So for people who have loved ones struggling with addictions right now, I just want to say a few things. All you can do is love that person. You can't make them change. Getting angry won't make them see what you do. But you can listen. That's not to say that you are responsible for their happiness, and I highly recommend setting up clear boundaries around how you interact with them. All I'm saying is if you think you're hurting seeing them like that, just imagine how they must be feeling while they're in it.

And for anyone who is in it, I see you, I know you're doing your best to keep yourself safe. Even if you're not where you want to be, I'm glad that you're here and I see that you're trying, and I believe in you.

One Year Sober—Essay

I waited for tonight to write my reaction to my year mark of sobriety. One, because technically speaking, it was like seven o'clock when I had my last drink. And two, because it's honestly a lot of emotion for me to process.

I had stopped drinking a few months before I got to the point that I did last July (clearly, that's how calendar's work). I had stopped drinking on a trial basis at first, with the intention of staying sober for maybe six months. Then it became a year. Then went back to six months. Basically, I was looking for an end date so I could just count down the days. I didn't do anything besides stop the actual drinking. I was looking for some way to numb the feelings I was having—drinking copious amounts of coffee, debating just replacing alcohol by taking edibles, playing video games for hours at a time. I thought that if I just took a break from drinking my problems would suddenly go away.

Clearly that's not how that works. But it was the first step that I took to helping myself, even if I was doing it for the wrong reasons. I was doing it for other people, because THEY had a problem with me drinking, THEY wanted me to stop, THEY were giving me ultimatums to stop. It wasn't about me. I didn't have a problem with alcohol. Clearly it was the other people who had the problem with my drinking. And that's why drinking was just a break-it was a concession for someone else to make it seem like I was trying. Like I was doing what I really needed to do and processing my shit and dealing with it properly.

The truth is that I hated the person that I was. I hated how I felt. I hated myself. I hated the times I lost control. And I was so afraid that if I stopped drinking and faced it that it would kill me. That even if I was drunk all the time, at least that was better than dying. Because, and this is the truth, I drank because I was afraid. I was afraid of my mind, my emotions, my life. I was afraid of myself.

And so I kept myself so numb that I didn't have to feel that fear anymore. I didn't need to fear what those things might mean.

I'm so sorry for everyone I hurt before I realized these things about myself. I'm sorry for the nights that I couldn't speak, the nights I locked myself in the bathroom, the nights I couldn't remember. I'm sorry for the fear that I had and the broken person that I was. And I'm sorry that I made that other's problem and not my own. When really I was the only one who could fix me.

This hasn't been easy. It has been a very hard year for many different reasons. But for anyone that is currently in that mindset... anyone that is currently so afraid of yourself that you can't see a way out of the darkness that you're in, that you just need to feel numb. To everyone who still feels a need to drink or whatever to feel okay. It's okay to be there. It's okay to feel hurt. It's okay to be afraid. I see you, and I know that you're worth working through this, when the time is right for you. There are people out there that love you and support you. Even when it doesn't seem like it. But at the end of the day, it's up to you to make the choices that you need to make for yourself. But don't think that means you have to do it alone.

Clearly that six months came and went, and I kept not drinking. And now it's my one-year mark. I have no intention to drink again. Maybe I will eventually, but I'm not planning on it. This is me now, and this is the person that I am happy to be. And I really am happy. I may hate my past, I may hate who I was, but I am happy with me. And I think I'd like to keep it that way.

Elizabeth

I was a boy of no more than sixteen, working as a footman at Sir Charles Damniel's mansion, when I first laid eyes upon my first true love—Elizabeth Damniel, Sir Damniel's only daughter. His only child. She was walking up the grand staircase to the second floor as I carried in a rather beaten leather suitcase that had just been returned along with my master from his vacation. I was walking through the main entrance, and she turned at the top of the steps and looked down at me, our eyes met, and I instantly fell in love, in the way only children can.

She was the most radiant being I had ever seen, with long amber hair in waves cascading down her back, and eyes filled with delight and intelligence.

She was also, I knew, dead for at least eight years.

It was a story that all the servants in the house knew, though I had thought them just stories to scare the poor boy who was new to the house and new to the career. The stories said that some days you could see the dress of the late Lady Elizabeth flitting around corners or hear the sound of brushing in her old room.

These stories started shortly after she had succumbed to the fever she presented in February of her sixteenth year, even after the lord paid handsomely for the finest doctors in the area to do what they could. It was not uncommon, but still sad, especially as the lord lost his wife when Elizabeth was born. Again, not uncommon, but sad.

She was gone a moment later, and I was left alone with my heart beating in my chest in the entrance hall. I set the luggage down on the hall floor and followed her up the stairs, but I found it to be as empty and quiet as the grave. Heartbroken, I returned to the luggage and continued my duty.

Repeating my tale to the other servants in the large mansion was met with disinterest at best, for they all had their own tales of seeing the ghost of the lord's daughter. When I spoke of the connection I felt between us, I was met with eyes that reflected the sad kindness of sympathy. I was told it would be best to forget her and continue about my duties and to not, under any circumstances, repeat this story to Lord Damniel.

And I tried. I really did. I kept to my work, with my eyes cast down at my feet, but I would still catch myself glancing up at the top of the staircase when I would walk past and would feel my ears perk up sharply at any noise in the quiet of the mansion halls. And at night, I would dream of her.

It was another week before I saw her again, my fair Elizabeth, with her lily-white dress and her pale face. I found her while dusting the reading chamber on the second floor. I was dusting the ancient and grim statuettes that the lord brought from Egypt when I saw her standing before the fire, staring up at the portrait hanging above the hearth. A portrait of herself or, at least, as she was while she lived. She wore the same dress in her portrait as she wore in her death, her hair pulled back and her mouth pulled into a soft smile. Her ghost did not smile, however.

"Hello," I greeted her, my mouth gone dry.

She turned and looked at me, her eyes softened by hopelessness. She spoke, and her voice was filled with the sound of bells and cobwebs and dust and song.

"Hello. And who might you be that addresses me and does not run from my sight?"

I bowed. "My name is Matthew. I am a footman for your father, miss."

"And are you not scared?"

"Terribly so. But I could not let you stand there alone with your eyes looking so sad."

She smiled and walked across the room toward me. "And what, then, do you think I have to be sad for? I have eternal life, it seems, walking the halls of my home."

"Well, it seems terribly lonely to walk forever alone."

Again she smiled, and if I had not already been in love with her, that smile would have done it. As it were, that smile is the thing I remember most about my sweet Elizabeth.

"Then, if you are not going to run from the sight of me, perhaps you would care to accompany me on a short walk?"

And, of course, I did. Disregarding the warnings of the other servants, I joined her as she walked the halls, her feet not quite touching the carpeted floors but rather gliding softly about half an inch above. And as we walked, she talked to me, talked as one does when they have not talked in quite some time, talking about every little thing—about artwork hung on walls, about the history of the house, about the places she played when she was but a child.

And I listened, as attentive as any to their heart love. And I was happy. And for those minutes, I believe, so was she.

After that walk, I saw her most every day, stealing away after my chores were done, doing nothing to draw the ire of my lord or the other servants. And I lived for those dwindling hours of the day that I would spend with my heart love, talking, telling jokes, being children. And I think, for myself if not for her, we appreciated the time that we could be children again, together.

On the fourth day since we had become friends, I was walking to her chamber when I heard the voice of Lord Damniel from the other side of her chamber door, and I realized that I was not the only one who had spoken with my fair lady these past eight years. I could hear them, their voices muffled by the door, but I could hear the tone of a stern father and the pleading, respectful voice of a daughter replying in return.

I did not listen closely to their discussion, for the words they were speaking were for family, and they were not meant for me. I did not want to intrude upon my love's affairs, and so I lingered, idly cleaning the same table down the hall from her door. And a few minutes later, when the lord strode agitated from her chamber, he did not notice me, and I heard his footfalls echo down the stairs.

I walked into Elizabeth's chamber and found her lying on her bed, her face buried in her arms, crying tears that never wet her pillow.

"Elizabeth, what…what wickedness has brought such sorrow to your eyes?"

She sat up then, drawing herself together and smiling through her sadness. "It is nothing, Matthew. Nothing at all. But you should leave… If my father finds that you have been talking to me, and spending time with me, he would be most displeased."

"And what if he is. I would rather risk his displeasure than to leave you alone in your sadness."

I sat beside her on the bed. Her gratitude radiated from her, and she threw her head into my shoulder, and her arm around my neck. Her touch burned of ice but was sweet as menthol, and I cherished it.

And with that she kissed me, which was equally as cold, and equally as sweet, and I was lost.

We enjoyed each other's company in this way for another few weeks, stealing off after my work was done to explore the dusty rooms of the mansion. Elizabeth, of course, knew a great deal more of the house than I, and we found the secret rooms unattended by the servants or the master of the house. Rooms that the two of us could frequent without worry of being disturbed.

It was during this time that I came to realize that the house was haunted, not by Elizabeth, but rather by her father, Lord Damniel, who would wander the halls on his own, spending hours keeping to himself and his thoughts.

I kept away from Elizabeth's room as often as I could, taking special care to make sure that I did not run into her father as we came and went. Twice I heard the two speaking and hid myself away until they were done, finding Elizabeth sunk into sullen sadness after he had left. I did my best to cheer her up as we explored the house, but even after our happiest moments, I would find her mood souring around the edges, could see an emptiness behind her smile. I tried speaking to her of this, as I cared for her and wanted to help in any way I could, but she kept it to herself.

And while we talked, I knew there were things that she did not tell me, some stories she would never tell, some emotions she would never express to me.

In those days, I started to recognize the difference in how the house felt. During the day, the mansion was quiet, dull, depressing. The air hung heavy, and the light felt as if it infringed upon the house, as if it didn't belong. Master Damniel would walk about the home or sit locked in his study while we servants went about our tidying or our cooking or shoeing the horses.

But in the evening, the house looked different. The torches made the walls glow and hid the dust. Elizabeth's laughter would mix with the evening breeze, and we sat together talking in front of one of the many large fireplaces in the house, my shadow playing across the walls of the old house. Elizabeth, of course, didn't cast a shadow. But we pretended that both of our shadows were mixing together in the twilight.

We were sitting in the drawing room just like that one night, the wind kicking up a fierce revelry outside, scratching against the windows and sending shrieks down the chimney. The dark had come on fierce and early, the sky covered in clouds so dark it was hard to say when twilight truly ended, and night began. But inside we were warm.

Or at least I was, I don't know exactly how Elizabeth felt. She didn't like to speak of the fact that she was dead, and I didn't want to discuss anything that would turn her smile.

But either way, we were sitting in front of the fire, watching the logs crackle sparks into the open floor, listening to the wind and the flames as they sang their songs. We had, perhaps, become somewhat lax in our protections of ourselves, as some of the other servants had begun to shake their head when I drew near, but I was too young and too in love to notice. Even if I had, I don't know if we would have done any different.

Suddenly the door to the drawing room kicked open, and Lord Damniel, covered in shadows and red in the face, bellowed at the sight of us.

He chased me down so quickly that I was unable to move, and his thick fingers wrapped around my collar and pulled me to my feet. Standing in front of me like that, he looked more a giant than a man, the fire reflecting in his eyes. I tugged at his hands, tried breaking free, but he held me fast. He was breathing heavy as he raised his hand, and I shied my face away knowing what was to come.

"No! Don't hurt him!" Elizabeth shouted, her face pulled back in anguish.

His hand steadied and, after a moment, dropped to my collar to meet his other hand. He shoved me away, and I stumbled but did not quite fall.

"You. You have betrayed my trust. You were not allowed to be near my daughter, and yet here I find you, you disobedient snail! After all my good faith in hiring you, in taking you on, in giving you a roof over your head, this is how you repay me? This is the thanks I get? Begone now, to your room, while I decide if I should release you from your position and let you sleep in the gutter. And you," he continued, turning to Elizabeth, "we have spoken of this, we have spoken of what you can and can't do with the second chance you have been given!"

"But, sir, please…" I wish I could say that I spoke with strength and authority, but it was slightly more than a squeak.

"*Go! Go now before I carry you from this house myself!*" he roared, and I scuttled from the room.

What more transpired that night between him and Elizabeth, I know not. For I ran straight to the servants' quarters and burrowed my head into my pillow until sleep overtook me.

I did as was commanded of me for the better part of a week, too afraid of what the punishment would be if I were caught in the presence of my Elizabeth again. I spent my days working on cleaning and carrying and sorting. Whether by the grace of God or by intention, my path did not cross Lord Damniel's path during these days, and I was thankful for that.

For her part, Elizabeth did not seek me out either, and I did not see her haunting the halls of the mansion. On the occasions that I had to pass by her bedroom chamber, I felt eyes upon me, but I never saw anyone, and I made my way past swiftly with my eyes downcast.

I couldn't tell you if it was love or grave stupidity that pulled me to her chamber and rap, rap, rapped upon her door on the fifth day. I'm honestly not sure if there's much of a difference between the two. But whether for a heavy heart or an empty mind, I found myself face-to-face with my heart love, her dead cheeks as pale as ever, spectral tears staining her face. Her face had passed through the heavy wooden door, and after a moment's surprise, she ushered me into her room, and I shut the door behind myself.

"You should not be here," she said flatly, keeping her eyes on the floor.

"Your father is out in town and will not be home for some time. I wanted to see you."

"He could have any of the other servants keeping a watch on you while he is gone. Even so... I am happy to see you."

"Elizabeth," I began. "Why does your father not want anyone coming near you?"

She hesitated, the same guarded hesitation I had felt during our evenings together. But after a moment, she began.

"He wasn't always that way. When I was young, he was the perfect father. Sad, after my mother's passing, of course, but he enjoyed walking the grounds with me after my lessons, and we always ate dinner together. He was kind, if not loving. And more importantly, he was happy.

"Of course, when I got sick, when I contracted the fever that took my life, he was worried. He paced the halls, never left these walls. He brought in all the doctors he could, but there's no way to stop God's will. At least not when it comes to the flesh. I for one was relieved when the fever finally took my life, for the weeks leading up to my death were a blur of pain and boredom. When I finally went it was...quiet. Calm. Peaceful. Far more so than the last few weeks of my life.

"But my father... One of the doctors he brought in was not a medical doctor. There were rumors he communed with the dead or had a pact with the devil. Rumors told by the servants in the house, of which whispers reached my father's ears. And so he came, in the week leading to my death, but instead of letting blood or giving medicine, he took clippings of my hair and trimmed my nails and took my favorite doll with him.

"When I died, I thought I was finally free. But I awoke, here, in my room, behind the grieving forms of the nurse and my father. I awoke cold and lonely. While you can see me now, more often than not, back then I had no control over it, and I was alone even though the house was still filled. Eventually, I was able to make myself seen, and when my father saw me, he cried and tried wrapping his arms around me...but to no avail. I think, in a way, it was him losing me a second time.

"But over time, he got used to how I was. How I am. He came to my room often, to speak, at first. For a while, it was like it had been before my death. But...death isn't like living. And the living, after a time, grow tired of the dead. As you, too, will one day grow tired.

"For one thing, I cannot leave the threshold of this house. We could no longer wander the garden or go into town. For another, I do not age. I have been on this earth for twenty-four years, but I will never grow past sixteen. I don't eat, I don't drink, I don't sleep... All I can do, sweet Matthew, is walk these halls. And for eight years, that is what I have done. Until you started to speak with me, and reminded me of life, I was nothing but a wraith in this house.

"And, I think, my father is afraid that you will take me away from him again. That if anyone speaks with me, it will reverse whatever curse it is that has tethered me to this realm. And he knows that I would leave, if given the chance. For I hate my life here, if you can call it that. I know not what lies beyond the veils of death, but it must be better than this. All I want, in the entire world, is to move on. To let go."

She finished her tale, and we fell into silence. Conflicting emotions gripped my heart—to want my love to stay forever, but also to free her from the confines she had found herself in. It was a lot for a sixteen-year-old to consider.

"Is there nothing I can do?" I finally broke the silence.

"You have already done more than you know, Matthew. The time we have spent together has been the best time I have spent since I died. Beyond that? Nothing. Unless... No, even then I do not know if it would work."

"What would work? What would work? Elizabeth, I swear that I will do anything in my power to help, anything I can to allow you to move on."

She considered me. I do not know what she saw in my eyes. I hoped they were radiating love so passionate that it might burn away her past painful years. "The totem that the witch doctor made…my doll with my hair and nail trimmings…if we were to destroy it, it may free my soul. My father keeps it locked in his closet. But if you were to retrieve it, we may be able to burn the totem and free my soul. But it would surely incite my father's wrath."

"For you, my love, I would sail oceans and brave the darkest forests. You father does not frighten me."

There may have been some false bravado in those words, and Elizabeth certainly noticed but still she leaned forward, and our lips connected again or as close as we were able to. And in that moment, it didn't matter that she was dead. I swear I could feel her heartbeat against mine.

And so we made a plan for the very next day, that I would steal away to her father's room, from the window on the second story, and retrieve the totem. I would go at midday, when the lord was having his lunch and would then retire to his study. After I had retrieved it, I would meet my Elizabeth, my sweet Elizabeth, in the same drawing room we had been accosted five days prior. And from there, we would set her free.

We were just finishing the details of the plan when we heard the Lord's heavy steps coming down the hall. For a moment, we froze, our plans would count for naught if I was kicked from the household before I could get into his bedroom. As his footsteps drew closer, boards creaking beneath his weight, Elizabeth ushered me to her bedroom window.

I threw open the sash and climbed through it, hanging from the small lip of the window frame, and looked back at her one last time. The doorknob on her door began to turn, and without further delay, I dropped the two stories to the ground beneath me, twisting my ankle quite badly as I landed on the hard, not quite frozen ground of late autumn.

Perhaps things would have happened differently the following day if I had not twisted my ankle. If I had fallen a bit more gracefully, perhaps I would have been able to move a bit faster and then Lord Damniel might not have caught me. But perhaps and maybes are for the young or poets, and I am neither anymore. And, anyway, the past has happened the way that it has.

But I'm getting ahead of myself. For the boy who scurried away from the window with a twisted ankle, that all was still to come.

The following day, I hardly focused on my chores in the morning, focusing instead on the location of Lord Damniel as he worked. He spent much of the day in his study, as was his custom, coming out several times during the day for food, or tea, but never once did he return to his chambers, and that gave me hope.

At last, he left his study and retired to the dining hall for his lunch, and I knew it was time to put our plan into action. I snuck out of the front door and walked around the mansion until I was underneath the master's bedroom window. With a breath, I began to climb the lattice work on the side of the old house, taking great care to not let my weight break the fragile wood and drop me. My ankle throbbed from the fall the day before, and I did not wish to add to the pain.

Eventually I reached the window and, with all the force I could muster with one arm, pushed the window open and clambered over the window frame. I cushioned my fall, but even so, there was a small noise when I hit the wooden floor. I froze, listening, not even daring to breathe. But after a moment where nothing happened, I stood up and began to walk through the room.

I found myself in the master bedroom, a large room that dwarfed the servant's quarters downstairs. There was a large mahogany poster bed, with white satin draping over the rails. A large chest sat at the end of the bed, and a large wooden bureau sat against the wall.

I found the closet and pushed the door open. With a creak, the door swung inward, and the noon light spilled in behind me, casting deep shadows among the hanging clothes. I began rifling through the shadows, searching, looking for the doll totem that might set my

Elizabeth free. I was so engrossed in my search that I almost didn't hear the jingle of keys opening the door to the master bedroom.

But I did hear it and had just a moment to dive behind some heavy coats. I could feel my heart beating in my throat as the door to the bedroom opened, and I could hear heavy footsteps walking across the floor.

Creak. Creak. Creak. I could hear the wooden floorboards squeaking as the feet walked into the room. There was a brief pause, and in the silence, I could hear my heart echoing across the room. Lord Damniel (for who else would dare enter his room?) could surely hear it and knew I was there. I scarcely drew breathe as I heard the footsteps pick up again, this time drawing closer to the closet. *Thump. Thump. Thump* went the footsteps. *Thump. Thump. Thump* went my heart.

After a time, the steps reached the door, and I knew I was caught. In a moment, I would be pulled from the closet, and Elizabeth would be lost.

And then the door closed. Simply and quietly, I was pitched into blessed darkness, and I heard the footsteps walk further into the room, pause again for a moment, and then leave. With a click, I heard the door to the bedchamber close, and I was once again left in the bedroom alone.

I stayed for several more moments, my heart pounding in the back of my skull, as I listened for any further noise from beyond the closet door. Eventually, I was confident enough to remove myself from my hiding space and slowly open the heavy closet door, pouring light back in to continue my search.

After several more minutes of frantic searching, I finally found the totem that I was looking for, the doll with the hair clippings tied to it with a thin strip of leather. There were markings in charcoal over the body of the doll, and the doll had obviously been slightly burned, half of the fake hair was burned away, and the porcelain head had warped and charred in places. I half-expected to feel something when I picked up the doll, some hidden power that had tethered Elizabeth to this earth...but it felt just as any old doll would.

My job now done, I tucked the doll under my arm, closed the closet, and walked to the bedroom door. I pressed my ear to the door and listened. Nothing. Peering through the keyhole, I was able to confirm what my ears heard—a clear hallway. A free escape.

I slipped through the door and closed it softly behind me, taking great care to avoid any noise. The door closed, and I turned and hobbled down the hallway, my swollen ankle shooting sharp pain up my leg with every other step.

Slowly, I made my way through the hall and then down the staircase to the first floor. I kept the doll tucked under my arm, but I was still lucky to not cross paths with Lord Damniel nor any of the servants. I walked as quickly as I could, which, to be fair, wasn't all that quick, to the drawing room where I was to meet Elizabeth and finally set her soul free.

Finally making my way into the room, I saw Elizabeth pacing in front of the fireplace, her pale translucent skin reflecting the flickering flames. She looked up when she heard me approach and smiled at me, the smile that tethered me to her the same way that she was tethered to the house. I smiled back. Then her smile dropped and was replaced with a look of fear.

I felt heavy hands wrap around my throat from the back. The rough, thick fingers of Lord Damniel pulled my feet from under me and held me high in the air. The doll, the totem which held Elizabeth in this realm, fell from beneath my arm and clattered to the floor. The world began swimming around me as I gasped for air, and then I felt myself flying through the air as Elizabeth's father threw me to the ground some distance from where I had been standing.

With a thud, I hit the hardwood floor, my lungs sucking in air, the world pulling back into focus around me. I saw, then, that the flames in the fireplace cast huge dark shadows across the room. No longer the sweet shadows of my days with Elizabeth. Sick, flickering shadows of myself, the chairs, and Lord Damniel played against the walls menacingly.

Lord Damniel towered over me, glaring down at my form lying at his feet, reaching with his hands outstretch. And in that moment, I knew he was going to kill me.

And he might have, if Elizabeth hadn't glided toward him, her arms outstretched and her voice pealing into a scream that was not of this earth.

"*No! Leave him be!*" she bellowed, her voice nails on a chalk slate.

Lord Damniel recoiled as if he had been punched. For a brief moment, the anger in his eyes turned to Elizabeth, and he raised his hand to strike her (though, what he would have hoped to accomplish with that, I know not). But in the next instant, the fire of rage died out of his eyes and glassed over. He stumbled back against the wall, as if afraid of his own mind, and after a moment, he buried his face in his hands.

We stayed like that for a time—me lying, breathing heavily on the floor, Lord Damniel leaning against the wall crying, and Elizabeth between us.

After a time, Lord Damniel stood upright, his eyes red and the shadows long across his face. He looked tired, then, and very old. Slowly he bent and picked up the doll from the ground and looked at it in his hands.

"I think I owe you an apology. Both of you. But you most of all, Elizabeth." His words fell out of his mouth, old and dusty.

"Father…" Elizabeth began to speak softly, but her father quieted her with a look.

"No. I have been…most selfish. And vile. When your mother died, I… I promised her I would keep you safe. It was the last thing I said to her. And when you took fever, I knew I had failed. I wish I could say that I did all this because of some secret promise with your mother…but the truth is I was just scared. Scared to be alone. To let you go… I never listened to you. I never listened to what you wanted. And now look at me…attacking a poor boy who was just trying to help."

I felt as if I was intruding on their family moment, yet I still could not move. Elizabeth stood before her father. And now he was openly weeping. Never before had I seen a man of such stature freely release his emotions like that, nor have I seen it since. But still he allowed tears to fall unabashedly from his eyes.

"Is this…is this what you really want, Elizabeth?"

"It is. It's not that I want to leave you, father. Please know that I love you and am so glad for the time we've had together. But this isn't life. I'm dead. I've been dead for a long time. And it's time for me to stop haunting this house and move on."

He turned the doll over and over in his hands, his eyes downcast, his breathing heavy. Eventually, he said, "Then I suppose we should destroy it. I suppose it's time for me to let you go."

And with that, he threw the warped doll into the fireplace. It struck the brick backing, shattering the top of the porcelain head, until it fell into a sitting position—one eye staring out at us, still smiling as the flames began to overtake it.

"I'm so sorry."

Elizabeth smiled.

"I know. And I love you." The two hugged, or at least as close as a ghost can.

"I love you too, Elizabeth."

After a time, Elizabeth let go and turned to me. It was the first time since I was thrown to the floor that either acknowledged me. I quickly scrambled to my feet and faced Elizabeth. She came to a stop directly in front of me.

"Matthew. Thank you. For everything. I've felt more alive in the past few weeks than I have in the last eight years."

"I don't want you to leave" was all I could muster.

"It's my time. Go have the most amazing life."

And with that, she placed her lips, pale and beautiful, on mine. And for a moment, for just a moment, I felt her in my arms and in every inch of my being.

And then, she was gone. The fire consumed the rest of the doll, and Lord Damniel and I stood without moving in the drawing room, our shadows playing against the wall as the fire slowly dwindled to coals. Both painfully alone.

I was released from Lord Damniel's home. He said that I reminded him too much of his mistakes and that it broke his heart. I suppose I understand that. But he sent me off with a small fortune, enough to set myself up with a good home and good work. I was comfortable and happy.

This all happened many, many years ago, when I was young. I am not young anymore. In my time, I fell in love again, fell in love and was married and had daughters of my own. I think I understand Lord Damniel now. I honestly don't know if I would be able to outlive any of my daughters. Or my wife, for that matter. I hope I never need to find out.

But even with all my years, and all my happiness, I still remember her. I still taste that last, final kiss. I still feel that childhood love. My heart love. My Elizabeth.

Happiness—Essay

Today I want to talk about something a bit different: *happiness*. And, I suppose, it's opposite: *sadness*. Really, just all emotions, I guess.

I've had a lot of people who have told me that I've gotten over things extremely quickly. That after only two months after my suicide attempt that I seem to have found my happiness and let go of all the sadness and loss and loneliness that I had been feeling. This isn't really true. I definitely still have those feelings. Honestly, in the last two months, I've felt sadness more often than I have in a two-month period of time ever in my life. The difference is that when I'm feeling that sadness, I can see a way out. I know that it's going to end. And I don't feel trapped in those dark feelings.

Negative emotions are a part of life. None of us can be happy every moment of every day. Honestly, none of us *should* be happy every minute of every day. Those negative emotions are what tell us who we really are, what we really care about. Sadness can show you what you really miss, what you care about that isn't there anymore. Anger can show you times when people are crossing your boundaries. Regret will show you the things that you've done wrong. And we can use these emotions to help change things—whether it's habits we have, situations that we're in, talking to people we haven't talked to in a long time. Emotions are our brains alarm system, and they're important.

But the important thing is to recognize that, while we have these emotions, we are not our emotions. We are not just constant sadness or happiness or anger. We experience these things. We feel them. We process them and figure out what they're trying to tell us. And then we move on to the next experience, thought, emotion, etc. Feeling them isn't a bad thing; it's dwelling on them where we create a problem.

The fact is that before, even in my happiest times, I would dwell on negative things. I would dwell on every problem, or perceived problem, from my past. I would dwell on words I said, words I didn't say, things people said and did to me. Even when I had everything I wanted, I still let myself fall into those negative emotions and set myself adrift, questioning my own emotions, my own sanity. And so I was miserable. More or less constantly. And I took that out on others. I blamed other people for my feeling terrible, as if somehow they were in charge of making me change the way that I thought about the world. That they were supposed to make negative experiences disappear. Which is flawed for two reasons: (1) good things don't cancel out bad things and vice versa and (2) no one else is responsible for how you feel. That's on you.

And the other thing I did, which I am now starting to really notice, is chasing the "high" of happiness, instead of happiness itself. I was constantly looking for a quick fix—drinking, playing games constantly, distracting myself so that I wouldn't think about anything. These "highs" feel great in the moment. You aren't thinking of the things that are upsetting you for a short time. But it doesn't set you up to find actual happiness. You aren't sorting out your thoughts. You aren't doing things that will actually help change your mood, like exercise or diet or apologizing. And you definitely aren't making the changes that you need to.

It's why so many people jump from drinking to smoking to video games to hooking up with random people in a bar and then set up to do the same thing the next day. But eventually those highs fade, and you're left right back where you were. Those problems are still there waiting for you. And then you feel like you need to do something again to try and escape them.

You see, happiness, real happiness, takes work. A lot of it. You have to be honest with yourself. You need to make changes. You need to do things that won't have results for a long time, possibly years. And you need to stick to it. You can't just make the change for a week and say, "Well, my life still sucks" and then go back to chugging beer while masturbating and playing Overwatch for six-hour binges. You have to stick to it. And even then, you aren't going to be "happy" all the time. More often than not, you're just going to be content. But content is still better than feeling like shit all the time, right?

So that's what I'm saying. Over the past two months I've felt sad, extremely sad. But I haven't let myself get trapped there. I'm working on things, working on bettering myself. That includes working on how I interact with the people around me, how I think about my past and the world, exercising, reading, working on projects, working on work. It has been work. But that work has been rewarding, and that's why I've seemed so different. Because I am. I'm changing and becoming a better person, the best version of myself. And that…that is where happiness lies.

Write You a Love Song

I've tried writing you a love song
many times before.
Something simple,
something about the softness of your soul,
or maybe the taste of your skin,
or the fact that you like smelling me.
I'm not very good at writing songs,
but I've learned four chords,
and about five different strumming patterns
and can kind of play with finger-picking,
and I'm good with words.
Night after night,
I slip my fingers over the strings
of first my electric guitar
and then my acoustic,
feeling my fingers scab over.
But night after night,
nothing sounds good enough,
nothing sounds perfect enough
to let you know that I love you more than
the pillow I've had since I was one
or that I carry you in my heart
even more than my little sister,
that I would allow you to lead me anywhere in the world
and be happy just to slide my hand over your shoulder every morning
to wake you up.
But I can't come up with the sound that fits that sentiment,
so my guitars just hang silently
on the wall.

But I'll keep playing every night,
misplaced chord after chord
and discordant note after note,
until eventually I find a sound that will tell you
what you mean to me.

The Travelling Flower Woman

She walks the earth,
leaving flowers beneath her painted toes
and crosses
concrete
and grass
and sand—
warm and restorative.
Her tongue is the taste
of new experiences
and spice of life,
as she continues to lay a line of
flowers
to mark her travels around the world.

I will follow the flowers
across the water,
across the cities
and the mountains
and beaches,
collecting the finest bouquet
I have ever beheld.
And as I go,
I will walk in her footsteps
and eat the food
and study the sky
so that I may understand how her soul tastes.

Love in the Time of Instagram Poetry

I cannot speak to you anymore,
but I can still sew words to my emotions
and put them down for everyone to read.
Words that show how I miss my lips on your tender skin,
words of our past adventures lost in the tall grass,
words that allow me to pour out the love that I still feel every evening
when I sit on our couch next to only the
shape that your butt made in the
cushion.
But maybe,
    just maybe,
these words will be shared across the Internet
enough that
your eyes will still see
my love.

Grow

What is life,
if not experience?
Do not let your feet
set in concrete,
for the tree without strong roots
will never grow.

Realizations—Essay

Things I've recently realized now that my mind is more clear:

1. I don't actually like parties. Honestly, they make me extremely anxious. Which is why I would always drink a lot at them to try to cover up that anxiety so that I didn't ruin everyone else's time. This includes my own parties, which is part of why the guest lists have dwindled more and more as time has gone on. I prefer smaller gatherings of people that I can connect to easier and where there isn't a ton of noise around to pull my attention in a million ways (note: does not pertain to concerts).

2. I lived my life in more or less a constant state of anxiety, honestly. Probably partially due to the massive amount of caffeine I consumed daily. I was constantly on alert for something bad to happen, just waiting for it. And every time the phone rang, my immediate thought was, "Oh no, what happened now?" And that state of anxiety slowly chipped away at every aspect of my life, keeping me distracted and fearful pretty much no matter what I was doing, making it so that I couldn't ever fully be present in any activity.

3. Related to the above, I kept myself busy constantly. Not sitting in quiet, watching shows and movies or playing games even in the middle of conversations. I'd be absent-mindedly playing games or reading something else to keep myself so distracted that I couldn't feel the anxiety, depression, or any other emotion I was actively trying to suppress. This was an extremely terrible coping skill that I developed and probably made it so that people didn't think I was listening to them. It wasn't true, even while doing something I was actively listening and cared about them and what they

were saying, but I can see where that made me look like an asshole.

4.   I can't eat pizza. This is probably more unique to me, but still. There have been studies correlating gut health to mental health, and I've found it's extremely true for me. For instance, if I eat gluten, I get super spacey. But I used to eat a lot of gluten-free pizza thinking it was fine, despite the garlic and onion on it. I've realized recently, using a food tracking app, that eating pizza actually makes me feel extremely depressed. So I guess it's true that diet is important part of self-care...

5.   My creativity is actually a lot better now. I don't know if the alcohol was distracting from just my focus or what, but the last couple months, I've had more creative ideas than I have in a while. And they've been better, more fulfilling ideas.

6.   I wasn't reading nearly enough. Recently I've been a lot more focused in my consumption of media and entertainment. I hardly watch TV or YouTube, at least as something I'm actively focused on. Instead I've been reading... everything from self-help books, comic books, novels, how to articles... And when I *do* watch TV or movies, they're specifically things I really want to watch, not just finding something to put on. It's felt extremely enriching.

7.   Having started meditation, I really notice how often I was living in my head, caught in the past or consumed with anxiety for the future. I notice things a lot more. Even just in my walk to work or at the gym, I've found myself more focused on what I'm doing and what's going on around me. And that's made me want to explore more, to go out in my free time, and to get lost and enjoy the city and world around me.

Just some thoughts about how much my life has been changing recently.

Myself

I know I wasn't always the best—
but I always wanted to be the best version of me
for you.
And now I am the best version of me
for myself.

New Words

I'm sorry that I can't write you a poem
about all the stars in the sky
or the red of the rose matching something in your eye
or speaking of angels or your body as a wonderland.
Those have all been said
by too many men
about too many other women
before.
I cannot give you some
recycled phrase
or worn-out image
to describe you.
You are too exquisite,
too intimate,
too YOU
to compare to anyone else.
But give me time,
and I will find new words
that have never been heard before
so that I may write you something
to match your soul.

Songbird

Songbird perched
on the edge of an electric piano,
her feathers glowing in the morning sun
as it peaks over the mountains,
her voice a low trill cutting through the early morning quiet
starting the day with love.

Oh songbird,
oh songbird,
wherever your wings should carry you,
don't ever let anything quiet your voice.
Oh songbird,
oh songbird,
how I hope that someday that song
will be about me again.

How Long?

I've known you
for how many years now?
All those years ago
in that windowless office
late at night,
dreaming of a future
neither of us thought
we'd live to see,
both cut in such similar ways,
waiting to scab over.

You've played different roles in my life,
and we've seen different worlds in our minds,
but still,
even now,
even after all these months,
and all those years,
it is you.
It has always been you.
And I'm sorry,
if I ever made you think
that it wasn't.

Thoughts of Suicide—Essay

I'm going to talk about something that I never told anyone before. I know that I *should* have, and if I had talked about it, then I might have lifted the power it had over me for such a long time…but live and learn right?

When those commercials talk about side effects of antidepressants, they normally say to pay attention to "thoughts of suicide." Now, I'm pretty sure when they say that, they mean thinking about doing it. But years ago, I started having visions of myself committing suicide as I was falling asleep. It was almost a calming thing, a reminder of escape. It started once or twice a month, but over the years, it started happening multiple times a night. I would just see myself hanging or bleeding out in a bathtub. There were times when it would go away for a while, normally when I was really happy and was able to pull out of the depressive episodes I basically lived in.

See, when I have nightmares, I never have nightmares about myself dying. They're never about someone coming after me or hurting me. They're always about the people that I love dying. If you're someone that's close to me, I've probably had at least one nightmare of you dying. And if you're someone really close to me, like a partner, it probably happened a lot more often than that. And those were nightmares. But the images of me dying weren't like that. They weren't quite sleep paralysis, but they were images that I just couldn't shake. And, like I said before, they had a weird calming effect on me that helped lull me to sleep.

But it was also part of why I was depressed all the time. Having those thoughts, just a constant cycle of dreaming of my loved ones dying and seeing myself killing myself over and over started getting into my head. It made going to bed a problem for me. So I started having problems with going to bed. I'd drink in the hope that when I went to bed, I could escape those thoughts (and it normally would, so that just reinforced that behavior). Or I'd stay up late and wear myself out to exhaustion playing games in hopes that I'd just pass out. But the worst part was that I would isolate myself in bed, roll away from my partner, and sleep curled up in a ball by myself to try to keep it within me, as if those thoughts would somehow poison someone else if I opened up about them, or that people would think I was crazy for having those kinds of thoughts.

But because I wasn't talking about it, my partner just saw it as me pulling away, mistaking my isolation as anger. And it was, in a way. An internal anger. I was angry at my mind, angry at the world for making me that way. Angry that I couldn't be "normal" or let the thoughts go. I was isolating myself just hoping something or someone would save me, and not doing anything to save myself.

It probably won't come as a surprise to many people that I've struggled with self-harm since I was a teenager. It comes and goes, the desire to hurt myself. Whether it's hitting myself, smashing my head into metal bars, or cutting myself… Whatever means it was, I've had large phases in my life where I would fall into patterns of self-abuse. I'm realizing now that this was a part of my communication issues… I didn't feel heard, so I started doing more and more intense things to try and show someone that I needed help. But I just couldn't find a way to talk about it properly. I was so ashamed of how I felt and that I wasn't able to be "stronger" that I just kept it all to myself. I've only admitted my struggle with self-harm to a few people in my life.

The self-harm had been better over the last few years. Largely because of my drinking. Because I was in a pattern of "survival." I was doing whatever half-assed coping mechanisms I had come up with to keep myself from hurting myself or from killing myself. As I've said in other posts, that included drinking, keeping myself distracted, putting on a persona that wasn't really me, keeping myself silent because of my concern about what people would say if they knew, keeping myself to myself because I felt that I was the only one I could trust. And I was so afraid that if I stopped any of those things, everything was going to hit me at once and I was going to be overwhelmed and die. And in my defense, that is basically what ended up happening. It was only at the last minute I was able to stop myself, with the help of my friends.

I'm not just surviving anymore. I'm starting to thrive. I'm working on my wounds, and I've come such a long way. I haven't had an image of me dying like that since a week after my hospital stay. I'm being so proactive about my mental health. Yoga, meditation, and working out have literally been lifesavers for me. It feels good to be alive, and not just surviving.

I know that in my patterns of survival, I did selfish and mean things, just doing what I thought I needed to do to keep myself alive. I know that I said things I didn't mean when people tried helping me see the patterns of self-destructive behavior I had built up. It's why when I first stopped drinking, I blamed the people that wanted me to stop. But I'm realizing the problem was me, that I was the reason that I had to stop drinking. Because I wasn't able to handle it properly. Because I was relying on it more than I realized. And when I stopped, it felt like there was an absence in me. And there was, but I wasn't filling it with the good things in my life. I wish I had filled it with you; that's what I should have filled it with. But instead I filled it with hatred.

I'm so glad to not be angry all the time. I'm so glad to be alive. I'm so glad that I'm actually thriving now, and not just surviving. And I'm realizing that keeping all this in had been a large part of why I felt like that all the time, so now I'm telling all of you, I guess. Make up for the untimeliness of it with quantity, I guess? Either way, thanks for reading! Have a good day!

My Bed, the Ceiling Fan, and I

I try to remember who I was
and why I thought it would be a good idea to be that person,
and I wonder why,
why
do I think it's a good idea to be this me now?
Not in a bad way.
I like this me now,
but I wonder what choices we make,
what choices we've MADE,
that build us into the people that we become.
Who will I be tomorrow?
I don't know.
All I know is that right now
I am lying on my back
on my bed as the sun goes down
and the ceiling fan churns the air
above my head.
Who will I be tomorrow?
I don't know.
But at least I know that whatever comes
I can find myself lying here on my back again,
my bed, my ceiling fan, and I.
And we'll figure it out.

Stars and Cosmos

I could have loved you like the stars,
but I was too busy drowning myself
to see the sky.

What is the cosmos?
Just dirt spheres spinning wildly
through space,
circling giant spheres of light
too far to reach.
Why, then,
would I look to the sky,
    when I can see so much more
within your eyes?

What Is It?

We're lying on the couch,
listening to Brian Fallon
plucking acoustic strings,
with the lights off,
waiting quietly
until the bad feelings
pass.
And if this is not love,
what is it?

It's 8:00 p.m. on a Sunday,
and I'm sitting in a smoky bar
listening to you sing the song
you were so anxious about
singing in front of the crowd,
but your voice is strong,
unwavering,
and full of emotion.
I could listen to that song every night.
And if this is not love,
what is it?

We're running,
half laughing,
half out of breath,
through the pouring New England rain,
down cobblestone streets,
and finding refuge in
a dress boutique.
While we drip rainwater
from our soaked clothes and matted hair

we kiss
and despite the cold rain,
I am warm.
And if this is not love,
what is it?

Taking care of you after surgery,
supporting you through your job changes,
meeting you for lunch every Friday,
walking through roses,
and reading in the park.
Is this not love?
And if love isn't what you need,
then what is?

One Year—Essay

Today is the one-year mark of my suicide attempt. The past year has been the most life changing and important year of my life. It hasn't been an easy year, but change never is. I started the last 366 days (it was a leap year, after all) in a psych ward. I spent three days in the ward after trying everything I could to convince them to let me go home. I'm glad they didn't. I'm not sure how things would have gone if they had.

But I made a decision then. I made a decision as I lay on the hospital bed in my room that I was going to change. That I was going to do everything I could to be better, the best version of myself. I borrowed a book from one of the nurses about emergency planning when you suffer from severe depression, and I made an emergency plan for if I got that bad again. It included reaching out to specific people, with their phone numbers listed. It included an hourly check in for my first couple weeks out from friends and family across the US. It included the list to the local hospitals and the suicide prevention hotline. I haven't looked at it in many, many months.

But beyond just an emergency plan, I decided to make changes in my life. These changes started in the way I think, from changing my mindset from being sober "for now" to being sober, to not just playing video games for hours to distract myself, to being open to new experiences and things that hadn't worked before, like meditation. And I took this new way of thinking, this approach that was "What do I have?" and not "What don't I have?" and used it as the foundation of my new life.

Since a year ago, I have meditated for at least 147 hours. That's almost a week of my last year spent meditating and getting to know myself. I've started gardening. I work out consistently. I do yoga. I sleep at a normal time (which was something I've had a problem with for most of my life). I upped my antidepressant medication and started an anti-anxiety. I started seeing my therapist multiple times a week, then shifted to once a week, and am now seeing my therapist once every other week (somewhat ironically, my appointment is later today). I started making room for myself, and most importantly, I started communicating (maybe too much).

I knew I never again wanted to be the person that I used to be, and that meant learning some things and unlearning others. I've read numerous books on meditation, self-care, communication, relationships, attachment styles, love, sex, and happiness. I learned about myself, my problems with myself, my problems in relationships, but also the good things about myself. I started writing again (I had been in a horrible rut with writing nothing of value for several years, which was both caused by and caused my depression). And the things I've been writing are some of the best things I've ever put down on paper, new themes and subjects that I never felt before.

And more importantly, I started feeling connected to the world again. To other people. To my friends and family. I was so clogged by my own self-pity and anger that I had shut myself off from those that cared about me. But now I realize that I was never as alone as I felt, and I can appreciate that, and feel that love.

I want to just make one thing clear, as it's a question that has come up a few times. I did not try killing myself because my fiancée left. It was more the opposite. She left because I was sinking so deep into my depression and my anger, and I was dragging her down with me. It wasn't fair to her, and I don't blame her for leaving. The man that I was wasn't the man that I should have been. I was angry and closed off and did not treat her nearly as well as I should have. I dismissed her concerns over my drinking and blamed her for when I would feel depressed because I wasn't drinking to quiet my mind.

No, it was quite the opposite. She left because me killing myself was an inevitability. I wasn't doing anything to stop it. I had stopped drinking but was intending to start again. And if you've ever quit anything, you'll know the transition into sobriety isn't easy. I lost my ability to escape my feelings, and they all overwhelmed me. I shut down even further, because coupled with the emotions I had kept bottled up was shame that I had let fester, and that shame was worse than I ever want to admit.

Honestly, that shame hasn't gone away, either. I don't think it ever will. This feeling of guilt stuck in my stomach that reminds me that I was the reason I was that way, I was the reason I drank, I was the reason that I never got help, and I was the reason she left. Like I said, I don't blame her, and I wish her all the happiness in the world. But that doesn't mean that I'm not upset about it. Because I am. I still am.

But I've continued living my life. In the past, in similar situations, I have shut down, cut myself off from the world, and got more and more depressed. I have enough friends who have seen me like that to know how bad it had gotten in the past. I would just keep myself emotionally dead until I found someone else to try fixing me. That wasn't the right thing to do, but I can't do anything about it now. So this time, I decided I would not repeat these mistakes again. I would work to fix them and actually face my demons, feel my feelings, and grow.

Honestly, if I had known what this year was going to hold, I don't think I would have stopped my attempt. The person that I was a year ago couldn't have handled the COVID outbreak, the self-isolation, the passing of my grandfather, the anger I felt at the fact that we still don't have equality in our country. The person that I was would have burned out and caved in and, well…probably would have died.

But I'm not that person anymore. I am me now. I am the best me that I have ever been, and I will continue to be that person. I will be all that I can and put as much love into the world as I can. I know there is nothing I can do to take back who I was, to take back my drinking or anything else. But I'll try doing what I can to offset the bad with all the good that I can.

For anyone struggling with their depression right now… I want you to know you aren't alone. Hell, even I still have to work at it. But there are so many people out there who are also hurting and who will be there to support you. It's hard to remember, it's hard to reach out, but just think for a moment. Think about the love you have. And hold on to that and let it replace the pain that you're feeling and talk to someone, anyone. Talk to me. Or the crisis text line. Or your family. Just talk to *someone* so you can find the best version of yourself.

I want to thank you all. All of my friends and family who have supported me through all this. Without you, I don't know where I'd be. But I especially want to thank John for being there for me when I called him this day a year ago. I want to thank Josh and Taylor for giving me a place to stay after I got out of the hospital. Nate who came with Josh and Taylor to the hospital the first day to make sure I knew I wasn't alone. To everyone that has talked to me over the past year to help with my shifting mindset. To my friends that I play games with every week. To everyone who has been there, thank you.

Here's to many more years.

Close

You're so close that I can smell you,
can feel the electricity from your skin
drifting up my arm,
causing the thin hair to stand on end.
Your kiss lingers on my lips,
and the sound of your breath echoes in my ears.
And I know you are there,
right beside me.

So,
then,
where do you go when I open my eyes?

As the World Ends

I always assumed
that when the world ended
it would end
with your kiss
lingering softly
on my lips.
But here we are,
slowly watching the world close down
shop by shop,
alone in our separate apartments,
with me slowly forgetting
how you tasted.

Happy Endings

I never
believed in happy
endings,
because all I've ever known
are sad ones.
But you've reminded
me of the joy
of a simple happily ever after.
For you I'd be a
Disney Prince.

Done

Afterword

And that's it. That's *Before/After*. This is me wrapping up the last year of my life and moving forward into a new chapter.

I'm not done learning and growing. That's still going to carry on throughout my life. I don't think I'll ever be perfect, but that doesn't mean that I'm not going to try. There are more things to learn, more people to listen to, more lives to live out there...and I plan to live every one of them.

Having gone through this entire book, editing it, reading it through multiple times, I'm struck by a few things. The first is that I was maybe a bit too critical of my earlier work. It's not as terrible as I remember. The second is the overwhelming love I have for all my family and friends who have helped me to this point in my life. I couldn't have survived the last year without you all helping me build myself back up.

And the third...the third is a great sadness for everyone who is still struggling in this. For all the people who feel unheard and angry and alone. The people who are told they don't have anything to be sad about or that get shut down whenever they try talking about it. Each and every one of you have the right to happiness, have the right to be supported and loved. It doesn't matter what you're going through. I hope you find the peace that you deserve and the support to wake up tomorrow better than you are today.

There are resources for you struggling out there. The national suicide prevention hotline number is 800-273-8255. Or text "HOME" to 741741 to get the Crisis Text Line, if you prefer texting. I volunteer at the text line and have seen it be extremely helpful. There are always people out there who care, even when you feel all alone. Your struggle is valid, but that doesn't mean you need to carry it alone. And I *promise* you, the world is a better place with you in it.

Even though my growth and learning will be a lifelong pursuit, this book marks the "growth" chapter of my life. The chapter of intense learning just to survive, just to grow, just to keep myself alive. I'm happy I had it, but it's time to move forward from that stage of my life, and to go on and live another. I'm ready for it. I'm happy for it. I can't wait to see what the future will bring. I never thought I'd say that.

Like Frank Turner sings, "The only thing that's left to do is live."

Acknowledgments

— Stories "The Monk Alone," "The Mother and Her Dead Daughter," and "Elizabeth" were all written for the Victorian Horror Troupe Phantasmagoria. They can be viewed in the archived shows on Phantasmagoria's Facebook page.

— Poem "A Walk through the City" was first printed in Brushings Literary Journal.

— Play *But What if it Was?* was an official selection for the Orlando Playwright's Round Table.

— Words from "Where Does My Body Begin?" were taken from the short film of the same name, as part of the compilation *Films Confiscated from a French Brothel.*

— Many of the poems appear in my first book *Obituaries for Terrible People.* But I'm too lazy to write them all down.

About the Author

E rik Keevan is a poet, playwright, and short-story writer currently living in Seattle, Washington. His work has been featured in the Victorian Horror Troupe Phantasmagoria, several short films, and published in several literary magazines. When he isn't writing, Erik is either meditating, gardening, or volunteering at the crisis text line. Erik is currently one year, four months, and twenty-nine days sober.